Family 360

A Proven Approach to Getting Your Family to Talk, Solve Problems, and Improve Relationships

By Perry M. Christensen and Benson L. Porter

McGraw-Hill

New York   Chicago   San Francisco   Lisbon
London   Madrid   Mexico City   Milan   New Delhi
San Juan   Seoul   Singapore   Sydney   Toronto

1 2 3 4 5 6 7 8 9 0 AGM/AGM 0 9 8 7 6 5 4 3

ISBN 0-07-142732-5

McGraw-Hill books are available at special quantity discounts to use as premiums and sales promotions, or for use in corporate training programs. For more information, please write to the Director of Special Sales, Professional Publishing, McGraw-Hill, Two Penn Plaza, New York, NY 10121-2298. Or contact your local bookstore.

This publication contains the opinions and ideas of its authors and is designed to provide useful suggestions on the subject matter covered. It is sold with the understanding that the authors/ publisher are not engaged in rendering psychological, medical, or other professional services. This book is not intended as a substitute for advice from a trained counselor, therapist, or other mental health professional. If you are currently in counseling or therapy, check with your health provider before altering or discontinuing your therapeutic regimen. The authors and publisher specifically disclaim any responsibility for any liability, loss, or risk, personal or otherwise, that is incurred as a consequence directly or indirectly of the use and application of any of the contents of this book.

 This book is printed on recycled, acid-free paper containing a minimum of 50% recycled, de-inked fiber.

Library of Congress Cataloging-in-Publication Data

Christensen, Perry M.
    Family 360 : a proven approach to getting your family to talk, solve problems, and improve relationships / by Perry M. Christensen and Benson L. Porter.
       p. cm.
    ISBN 0-07-142732-5 (alk. paper)
    1. Work and family. 2. Communication in the family. 3. Problem solving. I. Porter, Ben. II. Title.
    HD4904.25.C48 2004
    158.2'4–dc22
                                    2003019524

To our wives, Susan and Kerry, who have always known intuitively what we had to learn by hard experience: that no other success can compensate for failure in the home. We honor and love them for the husbands and fathers they are helping us become. And to our children, whom we love and cherish and for whom we want to live our legacy now—David, Brian, Breanne, Heather, Alyssa; and Kimber, Lindsey, Jayce, Scott, Jessica, and David.

Contents

Introduction

TO AN OUTSIDER, it probably looked like a clandestine operation. A pair of slick operatives would meet weekly in the early morning hours and talk in hushed tones. The times were regular—they would meet at 6 A.M. every Saturday in the local diner and depart at 7 A.M. No one else was usually up at that hour. The pair would talk and write things on the back of a napkin for an hour, then drive off in separate cars and disappear into the early morning light.

But it was just Perry and Ben trying to develop an idea that had been percolating for years. Perry had risen through the ranks of Human Resources at Merck, one of *Fortune* magazine's Most Admired Companies. It was also one of the most highly regarded companies for human resource policy, having been given numerous awards and recognitions over the years for its policies and practices. Most notable was its long string of awards as one of the top 10 companies for working mothers to work for. No other company had been in the top 10 so many times (12 years running at the time). Perry had lived outside of the United States for 6 years, living in Norway and working for

Merck across Europe, then living in Quebec and working across Canada. He had traveled a lot—usually 60 percent of his time. He returned to the United States to a corporate role reporting to the top HR executive and being responsible for human resource strategy and planning. Now he was responsible for ensuring Merck's continued track record in innovative human resources policy.

Ben had also risen through the ranks of numerous well-known companies: Lockheed, Amoco, PepsiCo, and AlliedSignal. He was responsible for executive development and worked directly with the CEO and executive team of these corporations, frequently in the capacity of an executive coach. At the time, he was the Vice President, Organization and Leadership Development for AlliedSignal. He had responsibility for all leadership development and learning processes globally for the corporation. In addition, he coached the executives on effective leadership and management practices.

Both Perry and Ben felt a growing dissatisfaction with the intense corporate life and the toll it was taking on their families. They had 11 children between them and spent much of the time away, returning to see how much their children had grown in their absence. Something was missing. They were trying to do their best in their corporate roles, but their responsibilities were becoming increasingly demanding. Both of them were overachievers and wanted to "have it all." They wanted success in both their corporate roles and their personal and family life. But how? Perry had spent years developing leading-edge HR policies, including work/life policies to help employees balance work and personal priorities. Ben had spent years teaching leadership and doing one-on-one coaching with the senior executives of major corporations.

Frequently, Perry and Ben found themselves providing one-on-one coaching on work/life balance to employees throughout their respective companies. Perry worked with groups of employees to discuss their feelings about what policies needed to be changed to make the company more effective. Inevitably, the frustrations and difficulties of trying to balance work and personal priorities would surface, often in emotional discussions that showed how much meaning the topic had for their lives. Perry discovered that company policies almost always fell short of their intended goal of providing some degree of work/life balance. And, in the absence of a supportive manager or work environment, the employee was left to his or her own skills and ingenuity to figure out how to achieve the elusive work/life balance.

Ben would frequently find himself coaching a member of senior management. He would assess the executive's leadership abilities and coach her or him on how to become a more effective leader. In many coaching encounters, the subject of how to be an effective leader migrated into a discussion of how to preserve the executives' relationship with their families despite the heavy demands of their work. Ben did not encourage that discussion—there were no easy answers that he could provide—but the conversation frequently just seemed to drift in that direction. Ben found that there was only one subject that would occasionally bring a tear to the eye of a tough, driven executive—when the executive shared his or her feelings of pain and regret for accomplishing so much at work, but at such a high price for his or her family and personal life.

So Perry and Ben decided to meet and compare notes. How could they have it all? How could they help others have hope that it could be done? The Family 360 process began to emerge, created on the back of a napkin. As the concept developed, Perry left Merck to do human resource consulting in a small firm, and Ben left AlliedSignal to do executive development with his own company.

The Family 360 process borrows its shape from the popular and effective corporate Management 360 approach to getting feedback from subordinates, colleagues and peers, and the boss—a "360-degree" approach to asking for feedback from surrounding employees, creating an action plan, and then doing something about the feedback. In Family 360, feedback is gathered from the spouse, children, mother, father, brothers, sisters, and others who have a close relationship with the person.

Ben and Perry began introducing the Family 360 concept to executives at some of the executive leadership programs that Ben ran for AlliedSignal, GM, and other major corporations. It was voluntary for the executive participants and provided a holistic and complementary approach to Management 360 and feedback. Ben and Perry refined their survey instrument and implemented an intranet-based survey and report generation process. A business was born, under the LeaderWorks logo (*www.leaderworks.net*) now based in

Monument, Colorado. The *Wall Street Journal* picked up on the idea and ran an article on the topic in July 2002. The *New York Times* selected the concept as one of the top 100 "innovative and breakthrough ideas for 2002."

So Perry and Ben decided to put some of their ideas and experience into a book, drawing upon the stories and examples of the hundreds of people whom they have personally coached and the thousands of people they have surveyed and interviewed one-on-one and in focus groups. All of them are people just like you. They love their families, they have strong personal relationships, and they love their work. They don't want to be without a strong sense of accomplishment in either area. But typically, the pressures of work in today's economy tend to pull their efforts toward work and away from family. The family can end up taking a back seat to the economic realities of making a living and holding onto a job.

Family 360 is about reconnecting and building personal relationships. It really is *not* complicated. It takes a little time, some tools for having good communication, and a little more information about what can be done differently to strengthen relationships. It is a process that helps identify where we want to be with our relationships, where we are currently, and how to close the gap between the two. In essence, Family 360 is the beginning of ongoing, open, and loving communication in personal and family relationships.

So . . . can we have it all? Perry and Ben think we can. That is what Family 360 is all about. It takes effort, perhaps starting to assess our family and personal relationships on the back of an envelope, talking a little more with family members one-on-one, and using the Family 360 approach to identify and make the needed changes.

Family 360

CHAPTER 1

It's Never Too Late

"If your wife and your children love you, you must have been good at something."

—New Jersey Taxi Driver

"Doing what's right for the family is never the wrong thing to do. Many successful people have achieved success at the expense of their most important relationships."

—Senior Executive, *Fortune* 10 Company

ROBERT CAME HOME from work uncharacteristically early that day. He remembers the spring afternoon, with the sun still high in the sky, and the warming prospect of spending time with his family. He had earned a little time off. His whole life was that of an overachiever. He had always worked hard— at first to pay the bills, and later for the gratification he received from succeeding at a difficult job. His career had been stellar by any measure. He had started off as an accountant, then gone on to more demanding management positions. Now, finally, as the number two executive of a 10,000-employee organization, the self-made 35-year-old millionaire was in a position to put all his energy and commitment into directing the company.

But it was not the bright spring weather or his satisfaction with his work or the anticipation of time with his family that he remembers from that day. It was not the recent buyout by a *Fortune* 50 company, which he had helped shape and which would help make his family comfortable for years to come. It was the interaction with his almost-3-year-old son that lingers in his memory.

He saw his son from a distance as he paused to retrieve the mail at the end of a tree-lined driveway that wound its way to the home. The boy was playing on the driveway. Robert could not see exactly what his son was doing; he spotted the boy just as his awkward gait ended in a stumbling fall to the pavement. Robert knew that the boy could not have hurt himself too badly—he was too short and too close to the ground to have done himself much damage. Nonetheless, Robert ran to help him. The boy looked up to see a man running toward him, calling his name. He instantly forgot his scraped knee and ran toward the house, crying out for his mother. Robert followed to see why the boy had run away. Perhaps the sun was shining in his eyes; perhaps he was startled by Robert's sudden appearance on the driveway. But his worst fears were confirmed when the boy nestled in his mother's arms, tightening his grip and burying his face in his mother's neck, refused to go to Robert. Robert's son did not recognize him. And he realized that, except for brief exchanges, he had not really seen his son in several months.

That was a turning point for Robert.

We spoke with him about the experience and how he felt. He talked about the serious talks he had with his wife, about his commitment to do something so that he would never experience that feeling again. But what could he do?

He realized for the first time that his work had interfered with an important relationship. He was usually gone in the morning before his son awoke, and he never returned until after the boy was tucked in bed. His weekends were eaten up with work and travel. There had been an occasional outing with the family, but that was before the big merger deal became a reality. Then he had dedicated even more of his time to his work for several months.

Robert realized that he had allowed his work to interfere with his personal and family relationships. "What can I do now?" he asked. "What should I do to reconnect with my family, my wife and my children?"

Robert's case is typical in our experience; he allowed the pursuit of success at work to eclipse success in his personal relationships. Equally common is the case of Scott, who worked in a highly demanding position with an equally demanding boss. Scott described the most challenging position of his career.

He was an operations manager for manufacturing and purchasing in a global high-technology company. "We did not have a day off in one year," he said.

I thought I hadn't heard him correctly. "You mean you did not have any vacation during that time?"

He corrected me. "We did not have any vacation, nor were there any Saturdays or Sundays when we did not work. And we were working up to 12 hours per day. The boss demanded it, and the work seemed to justify it. We all became sucked into the habit of doing everything for the company. Do you know when the turning point came? The wife of one of my colleagues had just had a baby during the middle of the week. He took a day off. Then the president decided to call a meeting on Saturday. That was not unusual. But my friend's wife developed complications—she actually was bleeding and had to stay in the hospital. My friend elected to stay at the hospital with his wife and newborn child on Saturday morning. The president was irate. He was angry that my friend had not attended the meeting. And then he justified his anger by saying, 'When my wife had a baby, I came to work a few hours later. That is the commitment I expect of my people.'"

"How did you react? What did you do in response?" I asked.

"First, I decided that I had a choice. I could do something about this. I decided to make life better for everyone in the manufacturing and purchasing areas. We began to take the long hours as a sign of inefficiency, not as an indication of high-volume demand, and we set about changing our work processes. We went looking for every inefficiency—and we found many and got rid of them. My people thought I was their 'savior' by cutting down on the workload, or at least sincerely trying to do so."

"And then?"

"While we were fixing our work processes, I was looking around for other companies and opportunities. I eventually left the company. I decided it was damaging my family life."

Contrast the stories of Robert and Scott with the story of Bill. Robert and Scott both realized that they were damaging their personal and family relationships. Robert realized that he himself was creating much of the problem; Scott realized that his boss was creating much of the problem. Both realized that they could do something about it.

Bill, however, was too late in recognizing the problem. I learned about Bill from his colleague, David, as we sat on an airplane. David summarized Bill's experience:

> Bill was the director of engineering for a high-tech manufacturing company. He had many prestigious and important assignments during his years with the company. Most recently he was responsible for the engineering program and the technical support for one part of the new space shuttle program. He had worked for the company for years, probably about 26 or 27 years. It was his life.
>
> Unfortunately, his dedication to the company resulted in some personal difficulties—he lost his wife in a messy divorce and became alienated from his children. He finally decided to retire from the company. He had earned it. He had the financial resources and benefits. He had the dream of doing things he always wanted to do. And then he died 6 months later. His brother made the effort to visit me at the company to ask a tough question. We sat down in my office, and he said, "Bill's former wife and family came to the funeral. But no one came from the company. Why not?" I did not have a good answer for that. Bill's brother had made the effort to come to my office just to ask the question. It was kind of sad that despite Bill's giving his best to the company, *only his family came through in the end.*

We have seen people like Robert and Scott throughout the world. And we have seen other Bills "in embryo," in their early stages of development. The same stories are repeated throughout the world, from the United States to Japan to South Africa, in thousands of well-meaning people who are dedicated to their families and want the very best for them, but who find the holy grail of satisfying family life frustratingly elusive. Some, like Robert, recognize it early in life, and some don't recognize it until it seems too late. These people come from every successful walk of life: police officers, doctors, librarians, teachers, business executives, and stay-at-home mothers and fathers.

Many of these people find themselves in situations such as these:

- They are starting a second family, and they want to make a success of it this time around.

- They are in a new relationship and a demanding new job, and they are trying to do both well.
- They are in a relationship in which there are heated disagreements about how to raise the children.
- They are in a relationship that seems to have stagnated, and they are starting to feel that they are "falling out of love."
- They are in a family in which the demands of work are complicated by the frustrations of raising children.
- They want to connect with their teenage children but do not know how to communicate with them effectively; this frustration is combined with feeling unwanted and unappreciated by them.
- They are working in a high-demand job, with high travel requirements that don't allow them enough time with their spouse and their family.

There are resources and hope for the person who wants warm and strong personal relationships and who is willing to invest some time over a long period. Any relationship, no matter how deteriorated and messy, can be repaired, rebuilt, enhanced, and improved.

So Where Are You Now?

You may be experiencing (1) a neutral to negative relationship with your spouse, (2) a neutral to negative relationship with your children, and/or (3) a general malaise in the family, or a feeling that your relationships are not quite what you want them to be, but you really can't figure out what is contributing to the problem. See if you can recognize yourself in these comments from busy people we have interviewed and coached. If you recognize similarities with your own situation, place a mark in the box next to that comment. Try to be as honest as possible with yourself and your situation.

❑ Stagnating romance

- "Once we got married, the flowers stopped. The romance and the fun have slowly, subtly slipped from our marriage."

❑ **Treating your spouse like another employee**

- "My wife says, 'Greg, I am not an employee. I don't work for you. You can't talk to me like an employee.' She says that at least once a week. For example, I ask, 'Did you go by the dry cleaners to get my shirts?' She says, 'No.' And I ask, 'You didn't get them today?' At work they would have done it if I had asked for it."

❑ **Giving your relationship with your spouse lower priority than other relationships**

- "I get up very early in the morning, go to work, and come home tired. My first focus is on the kids, and then I'm so tired that I crash. I don't have any energy for my husband."
- "I carve out this piece of time for the family. But I split that up between my boys and my wife. I didn't have a good relationship with my father, so I work really hard to have the relationship with my boys. And then my time with my wife suffers because I spend more time with my kids. She wants me to do more things with her."

❑ **Traveling frequently and inhibiting a strong relationship with your spouse and your children**

- "I travel a lot, and I was packing my suitcases for an international trip. I had a large garment bag on the bed. When I came back into the room, my 7-year-old son was lying inside the garment bag. I knew exactly what he was saying, and it about tore my heart out."
- "My wife and 4-year-old daughter were together when they saw a plane flying overhead. My daughter looked up, pointing, and said, "Daddy." My wife said, "Yes, there he is.""

❑ **Focusing on *activities* with children and neglecting listening to them and trying to understand them**

- "It isn't just about playing baseball with the kids. I do that. It's about developing a relationship with them. It's about talking and listening to them and understanding them. That's harder to do."

❏ **Trying to build relationships overnight rather than over time**

- "I will work desperately hard for 3 or 4 months. I will see my kids for only 5 or 6 days during that time, and then I will try to buy a relationship—I take them to the Six Flags amusement park or to the ballpark. And they think I am a great dad. I think I am fooling myself. I won't be able to do that when they become teenagers."

❏ **Experiencing impatience with children**

- "I come home and the house is a mess, the children have been quarreling, and no one wants to shape up. They don't listen to me any longer, and I explode."

❏ **Finding no time to create family traditions and fun**

- "The kids were doing a homework assignment for school that asked about their holiday traditions, and I couldn't think of any holiday traditions. That raised the question for me, 'What are we doing for our family traditions?'"

❏ **Finding that the family is functioning independently, without your involvement**

- "I feel left out of decisions, but I'm not there when they make the decisions. I come home on the weekend, and the family has already decided what we're going to do that weekend."

❏ **Experiencing a tug-of-war between work demands and family demands, with work usually winning**

- "I have not taken a vacation of more than 5 days with the family in years. I have 10 or 12 weeks of backlogged vacation. I feel guilty when I take vacation and think about all the emails building up and what will happen if I don't answer them."

❏ **Using a business approach to make sure that the family is focused on achieving their best**

- "When I come home, I usually go through this regimented, programmed business approach to asking questions: how my son did on his test, what my husband did when he got home, if the children have completed their assigned chores, and so on. And I haven't spent any time talking with my husband to see how he's doing. And I haven't spent time with my children to find out about their day and how they are doing."

Do you feel the need to change? Would you like some insights on how to address the problems that you checked off in this list? Now is the time to stop, regroup, and begin to work on the one or more problems in your relationships. In this book, we will walk you through a step-by-step approach to figuring out what may be causing some of your relationship problems and giving you an effective methodology for working through the issues with your family and developing some specific ways to strengthen and build your important personal relationships. First, here are a few preliminary observations from our Family 360 coaching experience.

Preserving the Primary Relationship

In our work/family coaching with busy people, we have found that the relationship that tends to suffer the most is the one with the spouse.

- "My husband and I do not get to spend much quality time together. We both feel that our son is our priority, since we both work and spend so much time away from him during the week."
- "We have two children, and we both have demanding jobs. My husband and I are just keeping our relationship on hold—we are not really building it in any way."

Typically, busy people will nurture their relationships with their children, but at the expense of their relationship with their spouse. Such people rely on the past strength of their spousal relationship and assume that the relationship will continue to be strong. Many treat their spouse as the caboose on the train of relationships. Most of the primary effort, energy, and time go to the children at the front of the train.

Unfortunately, efforts to nurture the relationship with children usually don't strengthen the spousal relationship, whereas efforts to strengthen the spousal relationship do have a positive impact on the relationship with the family as a whole. Too often busy people seek a solution in a way that works against them in the long run, continuing to ignore the primary spousal relationship in favor of strengthening ties with the children.

The second most common problem that surfaces during coaching is a general lack of feeling successful in family relationships. We have also found that in many relationships and in many families a general malaise sets in. *People are not necessarily doing anything wrong; they are just not doing things completely right.* In the absence of doing things right, family members may turn in other directions for fulfillment: to work, community service, or social circles. As a result, the proactive, assertive behavior that built the relationship in the beginning is replaced by "neutral" behavior. For example:

- Remember your second date with your current spouse? The time you knew that there was some magic between the two of you? You became proactive in order to build the relationship. You thought up fun things to do, fun places to go, and ways to enjoy each other's company.
- Remember the first time you watched your child take his first steps? You felt a wonderful love for the little, real person in front of you, and you wanted to be a part of your child's life and help her or him through the rest of her or his life. You couldn't wait to get home from work to see your child; you got down on the floor and played, and you talked for the first time in "baby talk." You exerted effort to build your relationship with the child.

Now, with these memories a few years behind you, you may find a certain level of boredom, a lack of excitement, or some malaise in the relationships. You may not have done anything to create a bad relationship, but you may have been negligent in building the relationship.

It Is Never Too Late to Improve Your Relationships

It's never too late to make a change, to build and strengthen family and personal relationships. All you need are the motivation and the tools to make it happen. Several years ago, when we were just beginning to create the Family 360 process, we were doing an in-depth executive assessment on a very senior-level executive in a large corporation. Part of the process involved interviewing a number of people who knew him well at work (e.g., boss, peers, direct reports, and customers). In doing such assessments, we also made it a practice to talk with members of the executive's family (e.g., spouse and children). We have continually found that much of what happens at work flows over to the family; it also works the other way, from the family to work.

This executive warned us that there were problems. He had spent many long hours at work, had traveled extensively, and had, in his own words, "sold his soul to the corporation," neglecting to take care of and build relationships with his family. We found that there was little left in his relationship with his wife. He had forgotten what it was that had brought them together in the first place. He had stopped working on the relationship and had allowed the flames of his marriage to go out. He had missed his children's school events and other special occasions. He had allowed a growing gap to develop between him and his children.

We had the opportunity to have frank conversations with both his wife and his children. It was obvious from these conversations that there was bitterness over the years of neglect. The kids were now married and had children; they had their own lives. It was hard for them to warm up to their father, to let their "absentee father" back into the picture. They did, however, suggest several ways in which their father could be more involved with their new families. We thanked them for their candor.

We couldn't help reflecting on how many executives we have worked with who gave their all to the corporation, only to find, when they began talking behind closed doors, that they had lost what really meant the most to them—their families. Many executives have expressed to us their feeling that their relationships with their spouse and their children meant more to them than what they got from the work world. Many who have made salaries in the millions have entered the closing years of their careers with regrets for having shortchanged their families.

It came time to meet with this particular executive and give him the feedback from his work associates and his family members. He had been very successful in his career. He had gone up the corporate ladder quickly. He had a strong reputation for getting results, growing the business, and building the capability of the people who reported to him. Then it came time in the coaching session to share with him the major themes that came from the interviews with his family members. It was hard to share these results with him. As we watched him stare at the table in front of him, we knew that he was hurting. After a few long moments of reflection, he looked up with moist eyes and asked, "Is it too late?"

Our answer to him, and to everyone, is that it is never too late to build, improve, and repair family relationships. It requires a commitment to breaking old habits of thought and behavior and building new habits that will strengthen the bonds of marriage and solidify strong relationships with children. That is what Family 360 is all about.

CHAPTER 2

The Family 360 Road Map

"Alice asked, 'Would you tell me, please, which way I ought to go from here?'
'That depends a good deal on where you want to get to,' said the Cat. 'I don't
much care where–' said Alice. 'Then it doesn't matter which way you go,'
said the Cat."

—Lewis Carroll, *Alice's Adventures in Wonderland*

THIS CHAPTER GIVES you an overview of the Family 360 process and the contents of this book. The overview will provide a useful structure as you work through the book and the exercises. The process in this book is simple, but effective. If you follow the process step-by-step, you will experience stronger and more meaningful relationships.

Any of the exercises that require interaction with members of your family and others with whom you have personal relationships will be of great benefit. In other words, any of the exercises will be very valuable in which you receive constructive feedback from those with whom you have personal relationships and in which you talk about how you can improve and commit yourself to an action plan and follow-up.

We also recommend that you implement at least one of the "big ideas" contained in Chapters 8, 9, and 10. There are hundreds of ideas throughout the book, but we have also selected and highlighted four "big ideas" that many people we have coached have found to be powerful ways of achieving stronger relationships. These big ideas have been used by many busy individuals for

13

years and have helped them to mend damaged personal relationships and build strong and lasting ones.

Will Family 360 help every personal and family relationship? The simple answer is no. There are many difficulties in relationships that stem from deep-seated psychological problems that may have more than one root cause. There may be a variety of factors and individuals contributing to relationship problems that need to be unraveled and sorted out. Many of these situations are best handled through professional care by qualified psychologists or marriage and family counselors. *Family 360 is not intended to replace the competent care, coaching, and close monitoring that many personal and family relationships require.* Family 360 is intended for people who want to boost their relationships, improve their communication, and make changes in their own personal life. Family 360 places the responsibility for and commitment to personal change squarely on your shoulders. So, if you want an upbeat way to start talking and relating to your loved ones, and you are committed to doing your part to make it happen, then Family 360 can be extremely useful and beneficial.

The Family 360 Personal Change Model

Family 360 is based on a personal change model, one that assumes that we are responsible for bringing about real and meaningful change in our lives and personal relationships. It follows a widely accepted approach to personal change:

1. Assessing our current situation
2. Identifying where we want to go
3. Creating an action plan to close the gap between where we are currently and where we want to go in the future

To implement the Family 360 personal change model, we need to understand where we are in our personal relationships—how strong and meaningful they are currently. We call this our *current state*, the status of our current relationships. We are in our current state as a result of a combination of inhibitors that influence where we are today: our work situation, our personal relationships, our social and community situation, and so on. There are many forces that are at work on us and that influence our direction. The direction may not necessarily be one in which we would like to be heading, but we feel locked into that direction, hemmed in on every side by forces outside of our control. However, the primary forces that influence our current state are factors over which we do have some degree of control. These primary forces are called *work inhibitors* and *personal and family inhibitors* (more about these in Chapter 3).

We also need to understand where we would actually like to be heading: the types of relationships we want to have and the ideal rapport we would like to develop with our loved ones. Perhaps we have experienced this closeness in the past and have felt it gradually deteriorate. Perhaps we have a favorite aunt or uncle or a close friend whom we admire who seems to have a wonderful relationship with others. Or perhaps we have never really had a good role model while we were growing up that would let us clearly and visibly see and know what a "good" or "ideal" relationship looks like. Regardless of our past experience, positive or negative, it is important to have clarity about where we want go in our relationships. When we understand the direction in which we would like to be headed and the types of relationships we would like to have, we have defined our *future state.* Our future state represents our vision of the person we want to become and the kind of relationships we want to have.

We should pause a moment and underscore that throughout the book we refer to *family.* We have used this term broadly to define *any close relationship that we consider to be an important part of our inner circle.* These are the people who are our best and most trusted and loved friends, be they our spouse, our partner, our children (by birth, adoption, or marriage), our relatives, our extended family, or even our friends. We will not mention this again in the book, but the point is not a trivial one. In essence, *family* refers to the people and the relationships that make life worth living, the people who enrich our lives or who make us better people just because they are closely associated with us. Similarly, we have used the term *spouse* throughout the book, but we recognize that some readers may have close relationships with partners as well, for which the material in this book is equally applicable.

Once we have a clearer picture of where we are and where we would like to be heading, we need to try to close the gap. Often this is difficult to do;

there are many factors that inhibit or oppose a change of direction and our attempt to close the gap. Often there are subtle habits of thinking and behaving that get in our way. These subtle inhibitors function essentially as "fog." We need to understand some of the fog that distorts and hides where we are and where we want to be going. We will describe the most common and pervasive reasons that people seem to lose track of their destination. The fog is a result of some *patterns of thinking* that are deeply ingrained and some *patterns of behaving* that are firmly entrenched—and the way in which these patterns of thinking and behaving reinforce each other. This sounds complicated, but it really is not. If we persist in getting lost in the "thinking fog" and the "behavioral fog," we will continue to experience difficulty in getting to where we want to be heading. Frequently, we are so lost in our thinking fog and behavioral fog that we do not even realize that we are lost or headed in the wrong direction.

To clear out the fog, there are some basic principles of thinking and behaving that we need to start doing more consciously. These principles, when acted upon, will help us achieve our future state in two ways: 1) We will have greater clarity about where we want to be with our personal relationships; 2) these principles will also help us close the gap between our current and future state. We will be able to eliminate practices that inhibit our movement toward our future state and to acquire practices that help drive us forward in the right direction. These thinking and behaving principles need to be the foundation for how we interact with people we love.

To help close the gap and accelerate our progress along the path to our future state, we first need to more aggressively focus on the many things we do correctly. We frequently underestimate the power of building on and leveraging our current strengths. And we all have strengths—even the most grumpy, interpersonally inept, and cantankerous person among us. There are always things that we do right and things that *others* see us as doing right, but *we* may not see it. Perhaps we are overly critical of our own actions. Perhaps we have always held ourselves to a higher standard. Or perhaps we can see only the bad things we do in our relationships because the people close to us remind us of what we are doing wrong. We all have strengths—some of us just have to look harder for them than others.

In addition, we frequently have strengths that we do not leverage fully. For example, we may be a good coach and mentor at work but may not apply that strength in our family. We may be patient with our children but not apply that strength to our spouse. We may be compassionate and service-oriented with our elderly parents but not apply that strength to our teenage children. In summary, we need to identify and leverage our strengths to build our personal and family relationships.

Once we have identified and leveraged our current strengths to move us toward our future state, we need to identify other ways to close the gap. There are things we can do to help us close the gap by building new ways of behaving into our habits. These *three pillars of behavior* help to *support and sustain* our efforts to stay on track. The three pillars are "core behaviors, relationship behaviors, and growth behaviors." People who want to have stronger relationships need to establish a baseline degree of proficiency in each pillar of behavior. The Family 360 survey will provide you with a list of key questions to help you assess how well you are doing in the three behavioral pillars and what needs to improve. In addition, we will provide you with a wealth of best practices that other busy people have used to become better at these key behaviors and close the gap.

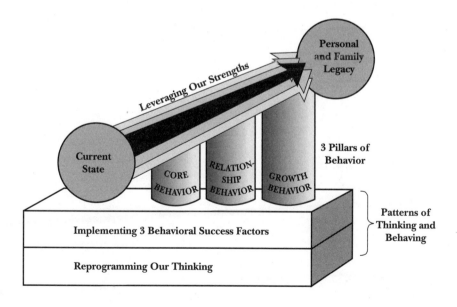

This is the complete model for Family 360. It boils down to understanding where we are, where we want to be headed, and how to get there. It involves reshaping some of our thinking and behaving as a foundation for better relationships. And it involves continuing to do things that we already do well (building on our strengths) and identifying and implementing a few things that will improve those areas where we are weak. Most important, it involves having an ongoing conversation with our family and others with whom we have personal relationships so that they can help us become better.

Throughout the book, we will be providing you with exercises. Some of these exercises are meant for self-reflection; others are meant to provide you with solid data and information on how to improve your relationships, along with opportunities to initiate meaningful conversations with your spouse and family members.

CHAPTER 3

Think Your Way into a New Way of Behaving

"If your success is not on your own terms, if it looks good to the world but does not feel good in your heart, it is not success at all."

—Anna Quindlen

THE FAMILY 360 Personal Change Model helps us identify where we are currently (our current state), where we want to go (our future state), and how we can effectively close the gap between where we are and where we want to be. The first step in closing the gap is to identify some common flaws in our thinking—flaws that can inhibit our achieving what we really want in our relationships.

EXERCISE: *How Would You Define "Success"?*

Much of the way we view the world and our lives and the way we subsequently act is based on how we feel we can best achieve success. But what is "success"? Think for a moment about how you would define success. When you think about being successful in life, how do you picture your achievements and accomplishments?

Without too much thought, write down the answers to the following questions. Take a minute or two to answer each question.

1. How do you define success?

2. List eight to ten of your achievements you have had throughout your life.

Take a quick look at your definition of success and your list of achievements, and ask yourself two simple questions:

- To what extent do my answers include words that describe success and achievement within my work or occupation?
- To what extent do my answers include words that describe success and achievement in my personal and family relationships?

We have found that busy people around the globe tend to have one common characteristic: They tend to define their success in terms of their professional and work achievements. When they look in the mirror of success, they tend to focus on how they are seen as a worker, boss, or owner, rather than on how they are seen as a husband, wife, father, mother, brother, sister, and so on. When they think of success, they define themselves by their achievements in the workplace rather than by their achievements in their home.

Perhaps you have a strong focus on your personal and family relationships. However, many of the people we have coached have an internal drive mechanism with a heavier focus on success within their chosen occupation. They channel their energies, commitment, and time into making themselves successful in their work. Behind many definitions of success are words that indicate an interest in pursuing career success over success in other primary relationships. For example, we find the following trends among busy, achievement-oriented people:

- If they have been recognized for being successful as an individual contributor, they would like to become a manager of people.
- If they work at a manager level, they would like to achieve a vice president level.
- If they have reached a certain salary level, they would like to reach a greater salary level, and perhaps become independently wealthy.
- If they work in a *Fortune* 500 company, they would like to move up to work in a *Fortune* 10 company.
- If all of their experience has been inside the United States, they would like to acquire global experience.

These are not bad goals—unless they become our primary goals.

We all base our thinking patterns, our way of thinking, on our experiences. Frequently, our way of thinking is firm and established. Think of a fortress or a stronghold. There are high stone walls that cannot be climbed, a narrow entryway that is well protected and guarded, and a sentry who overlooks the outside and warns of impending danger. It is a structure that is built to protect what is inside and keep it safe from what is on the outside. It can be difficult to enter or breach. Our minds and our way of thinking are very much like the stronghold. We have our own personal "mindhold," a solid structure that is difficult to breach. We have built up our mindhold on the basis of our experiences, to protect our way of thinking and our paradigms or ways of looking at things.

As we try to achieve success in our personal and family relationships, we frequently think in ways that prevent us from fully developing those relationships. As we are caught up in the pressures of earning a living and putting food on the table, we frequently evaluate our success in life on the basis of our work success and the way others view, recognize, and reward our work. We call this habit of thinking *thinking fog* because it obscures, masks, or minimizes the *need* for thinking or behaving in a more effective way.

Traveling through such thinking fog on our road to success is actually quite natural. We all experience it to varying degrees at different times in our lives. Often we define success as accomplishment at work because we are visibly, openly, publicly acknowledged for our work achievements. We work hard and are recognized with promotions, advancement opportunities, pay, and so on. Success in our family is not as openly recognized and acknowledged. When we are a good spouse, we don't receive open acknowledgment of our abilities or open recognition. We don't receive a plaque, an award, a promotion, or a larger paycheck. When we are a good parent, we are usually not recognized with more than the annual Mother's Day pencil can or the Father's Day paper tie.

Overcoming Thinking Fog

Success in our personal and family relationships can accelerate as we change both our way of thinking *and* our way of behaving. The process is cyclical. A new way of thinking can help us change our behavior. Experimenting with new behavior can help us change and reprogram our way of thinking. In fact, we can dramatically accelerate change in our personal and family relationships if we work on our thinking and our behaving simultaneously.

There are two points of entry into this cycle of successful personal and family relationships. A point of entry is a point where we introduce significant personal change by introducing *new ideas and thinking* or introducing *new behavior* into our cycle of thinking and behaving. We will discuss the point of entry for *behavior* in the next chapter; however, in the remainder of this chapter we discuss how to begin to change our *way of thinking*.

Our first step toward successful personal and family relationships is to create a different way of thinking and to cut through the thinking fog. As we start to think about our thinking, we begin the process of closing the gap between where we are and where we want to go. And the examination of our thinking starts with having a serious inner conversation about:

1. ***Rebalancing our definition of success.*** We need to redefine success, broadening our definition to include ways in which we can achieve success in our personal and family relationships.
2. ***Reprogramming our power of choice.*** We need to recognize that we have more influence over our personal situation and how we respond to it than we currently acknowledge.

Both of these ways of thinking are entry points or catalysts for changing and recharging our thinking, as the diagram illustrates. Both ways of thinking help cut through the thinking fog.

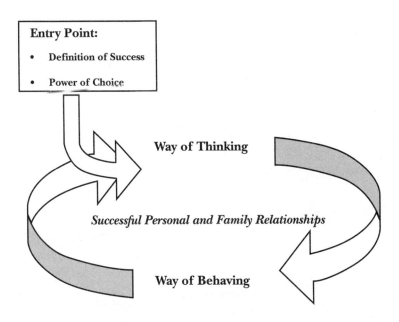

EXERCISE: *Rebalancing Your Definition of Success*

A senior-level executive in a major corporation described how she had had to abruptly adjust her definition of success:

> I was diagnosed with thyroid cancer. That was a shock in and of itself. But can you imagine how I felt when the doctor, in questionable bedside manner, told me that I should make a list of the top ten things I hadn't done in my life that I wanted to do? After I got over the shock of hearing the news, I decided to follow the doctor's advice. The interesting thing was that eight out of the ten things had nothing to do with work.

> While success is usually attributed to our work efforts, what is really important? Take a few minutes to answer the following questions and contrast your answers with the answers to the previous questions on success.

1. If I had only 3 years to live, what ten things would I like to accomplish during that time?

2. I am at my best when . . .

3. I am truly happy when . . .

4. At my funeral service, I would like people to say this about me:

5. I want to be a person who . . .

6. My deepest positive emotions come when . . .

7. When all is said and done, the most important things are . . .

    Notice how, in your answers to these questions, you have redefined success in terms of personal relationships. We have found that *individuals need to redefine success—not to exclude their work success, but to include success in their relationships with family members.* Success in family relationships needs to become a way of thinking, a new paradigm for how we look at ourselves and our achievements, and to be fully integrated with our success at work. Another major purpose of Family 360 is to help individuals establish and reinforce a process of rebalancing—of looking at family and personal relationships as the core element of personal success.

    This rebalancing is analogous to rebalancing a sailboat in turbulent seas, as Perry's experience illustrates.

> My wife and I were recently on a sailboat off the coast of Maui. We were enjoying a delightful day of sun and gentle breezes. The boat was built for speed, and the sails were fully unfurled to skim us rapidly over the water. Shortly after noon, without warning, the wind picked up and started blowing us away from our harbor destination; an afternoon

squall threatened. We tried heading for shore, but the waves became larger and the wind more treacherous. The onboard motor became useless as a source of power, as each wave pitched the boat so that the propeller came out of the water. The sails strained at the wind, and the boat leaned at a 45-degree angle to the sea. Had my wife and I been piloting the boat ourselves, we would have been halfway to Tahiti before anyone noticed that we were gone.

But our shipmates knew how to deal with the situation by rebalancing the boat. First, they pointed the boat into the wind toward our destination. Next, they lowered all but a few sails and used the power of the wind to gradually bring us to the harbor. Rebalancing the boat involved two factors:

1. Underneath the boat, hidden from view and quietly working, was the keel. The keel acted as a restraining force in the water and prevented us from capsizing. The boat leaned heavily to the side and appeared dangerously out of balance, but, in fact, it was in *perfect* balance. The keel provided the underlying foundation that kept the boat directed toward our goal and in balance despite the threatening storm. Our friends knew the value of the keel during turbulent weather and relied on its stabilizing force.
2. The crew immediately reduced the surface area of the sails and maneuvered them to just the right angle to get the proper pull from the wind. The sails that had had us skimming along at high speed just a few minutes earlier would have tipped us over into the water had the crew not managed to trim the sails and rebalance us quickly.

How does the behavior of a sailboat in stormy seas apply to us? At times in our busy work and personal lives we get caught up in the thrill of the wind carrying us along. The thrill that we get from our work is important. It provides us with great satisfaction and challenge. It is a necessary part of life and perhaps needs only minor rebalancing.

However, we occasionally journey through some fairly challenging times and face some winds of adversity. When times get difficult and we feel stormy weather approaching, then we need to reassess and rebalance. Most of us forget the powerful stabilizing effect of our own "keel," our own beliefs, values, and priorities. We forget how much our family and personal relationships have contributed to our sense of self and our sense of values. But we will weather the storm if we shift and rebalance ourselves, recognizing and focusing more on the stability of family and personal relationships and less on the thrill of our work achievements. We can actually be in balance even when the world around us is in turmoil and work pressures are mounting if we rely on the stabilizing force of our relationships. A tipping point won't come if we are well grounded. Our experience in work/life coaching reinforces the idea that in difficult times (and also in good times), success has to be balanced. Otherwise, we end up like Bill in the first chapter who, because of a focus exclusively on work, lost connection with his family, the only ones who truly cared about him.

Rebalancing begins with the mental recognition that *our family relationships are at the core and foundation of who we are.* We recondition ourselves as we retune our thinking to include family and personal relationships in our definition of success. We will help you further develop this pattern of thinking in Chapter 5 as we walk you through an exercise to create your own written "family legacy"—how you want to be remembered and what you want as your lasting contribution to your personal relationships.

Reprogramming Our Power of Choice

Robert from Chapter 1 took a hard look at his life and did not like what he saw. He realized that he was not balanced in his priorities and in the way he thought about personal success. However, he was not sure he could do anything about it. He had a long and frank discussion with his wife about what he could do to resolve the situation and still do well at work. Together, they thought through how important their family relationships were to Robert and how they would like to shape their family relationships in the future. They came up with a plan of action that included several changes at work and at home that would close the gap between where he wanted to be and where he was currently:

- *At work.* Robert spoke with his boss about his dilemma and asked that his boss evaluate him only on his results. At first the boss was skeptical, but he made a commitment to allow Robert more latitude and flexibility in managing his work priorities. Second, Robert created a calendar for his work group that showed the critical work project milestones, but also included critical personal events that he did not want to miss or compromise—his son's birthday party, his wedding anniversary, a social event at the synagogue, and so on. And he allowed the other members of the department to write into the calendar the critical personal milestones that they did not want to miss. They integrated their important personal events into the work schedule and created an open atmosphere in the department that gave everyone permission to discuss important personal events.

- *At home.* Robert spent more time with his son. He called him on the phone during the day just to chat for a few minutes. He came home earlier several days a week and finished his work in the evening after his son was in bed. And he made specific commitments to be with his son for planned fun activities and for important events—commitments that he tried hard not to break.

In summary, Robert rebalanced his thinking about what made him successful. In addition, he realized that he had more choice than he had originally thought; he could do something to put into practice his new thinking about success. He did not feel totally free, but there were some things that he could choose to do differently at work and some that he could choose to do differently at home. He thought his way into a new way of behaving.

Let's be realistic. Rebalancing your thinking about success is difficult. Many people have asked, "How can I be successful in my personal relationships with so much against me? How can I rebalance my life when I have no control over my life?" There are many factors outside of our control that contribute to our feelings of inadequacy and powerlessness. As coaches, we continually hear about the difficulties and challenges people face in having successful relationships. These challenges are real and tough and debilitating.

Over time, they wear people down. They tire people and sap their energy as well as discourage, demotivate, and immobilize them.

Let's take a look at the top 17 inhibitors that lead people to become immobilized and discouraged, which in turn leads to stagnation and deterioration in their personal relationships. We will do this with a simple exercise that will allow you to assess what hurts your personal relationships. These top 17 inhibitors are derived from what has surfaced during our coaching and generally fall into two categories:

- Work inhibitors
- Personal and family inhibitors

EXERCISE: *What Are the Primary Inhibitors That Contribute to Your Stagnating or Deteriorating Personal and Family Relationships?*

Through our work, we have identified the top inhibitors that contribute to stagnating or deteriorating personal and family relationships. These inhibitors oppose or limit our drive toward our future state. The purpose of this exercise is to identify the main elements in our work and personal life that influence and inhibit our ability to achieve our future goals. When we have identified these inhibitors, we can begin to work on them, to change and minimize them. Each contributor is illustrated with comments and actual examples.

As you review the examples, circle the number in the box in the lower right-hand corner of each that most closely represents the frequency with which that inhibitor occurs in your life. For example, your work schedule may require you to work overtime (a potential cause of deteriorating personal and family relationships) either (4) almost all the time, (3) frequently, (2) occasionally, or (1) almost never. Your numerical value will be used later to calculate your final score.

Top Nine Work Inhibitors

1. Organizational Culture That Encourages Long Hours More than Results

- "Everyone knows that the promotion goes to the person who works the longest hours. What it all boils down to is this: When there is a promotional decision, with all else equal, the person who works 60 hours is going to get the job over someone who works 40 hours, even if the person who works fewer hours is actually more efficient. That means my family suffers."

- "I had been consistently working 12-hour days, 6 days a week. I planned a weekend trip with my family and then had to cancel the trip to complete a project. My manager told me, 'As you go up the promotion ladder in the company, your personal life will shrink.' It is really irritating that he never acknowledges or even recognizes the previous sacrifice and the continual long work hours I've been putting in."

- "Part of the problem is that performance is measured by how many hours you put in. If you're putting in lots of hours, you must be working hard."

- "There's a 'badge of honor' for those who work long hours. You're seen as a hero. We reward the heroes who put in more hours, but the person who leaves at 5 P.M. may be doing a better job."

Assess *Your* Situation:	Frequency: (Circle One)			
The culture of the company requires me to work long hours and to focus all my time and energy on my work.	**4** Almost All the Time	**3** Frequently	**2** Occasionally	**1** Almost Never

2. Last-Minute Requests by Management

- "A request was made for information at the very last minute of the work day. I had to stay two extra hours. I brought my young son over from the day-care center, sat him down on the floor next to me and fed him crackers, and did the analysis. I had previously recommended a very targeted analysis. But I was told to do the analysis every possible way, even though the president probably needed only one analysis done. My manager was afraid to ask the question to find out (or to recommend) what was specifically needed. So my son and I ended up making a sacrifice."

- "My manager likes to create crises in our work that result in longer hours and more last-minute fire fighting. The entire culture of the company is one of fire fighting at the last minute. The organization determines the level of importance of an issue by the amount of crisis it creates—if there is a crisis, then it must be important. But that means our families frequently bear the brunt of the crisis."

Assess *Your* Situation: My manager asks employees to do last-minute work that results in more time away from home.	**Frequency: (Circle One)**			
	4 Almost All the Time	**3** Frequently	**2** Occasionally	**1** Almost Never

3. Pressure from the Work Team

- "There is a very real pressure to contribute to the team. I feel guilty if I ever have to leave work early for a personal reason, particularly if everyone else on the team is still at work. My team takes up the slack."
- "You're supposed to take child care leave, but it puts stress on your colleagues. I feel a subtle pressure to return quickly."
- "People on my team make me feel guilty for taking holidays or vacation. They feel that everyone has to sacrifice for the good of the team."

Top Nine Work Inhibitors (*continued*)

Assess *Your* Situation:	Frequency: (Circle One)			
My team at work is under pressure to produce, and I feel guilty when I don't put in as much time as the others on my team do.	**4** Almost All the Time	**3** Frequently	**2** Occasionally	**1** Almost Never

4. Management Discouragement of Attending to Personal Needs

- "I was told by my boss that she wouldn't have hired me if she had known I was going to have a child. She wanted someone who could make a long-term commitment to the job."

- "There is a well-known saying in [this] department of the government: 'If we wanted you to have a family, we would have issued you one.'"

- "One manager comes in all the time, even when sick. One time the manager came in for an entire week with bronchitis. The secretary ended up getting sick and had to be out for 2 days. Employees say they feel guilty when they have to take sick time off because of the manager's approach."

- "All the employees know that the CEO spent his Christmas day working on and approving the compensation plan for the next year."

- "The vice president was making calls from the hospital just prior to delivering her baby. Everyone knows she took her cell phone into the delivery room with her. That is the kind of commitment she expects from everyone."

Assess *Your* Situation:	Frequency: (Circle One)			
Management subtly and sometimes explicitly discourages employees from spending time on personal relationships.	**4** Almost All the Time	**3** Frequently	**2** Occasionally	**1** Almost Never

5. Management Insensitivity to People Needs

- "I put in 200 hours of overtime over the course of 2 months. I was pregnant at the time, and I had to schedule 3 hours during work for

Top Nine Work Inhibitors (*continued*)

an ultrasound appointment. When I asked the manager for the time off, well ahead of the ultrasound appointment, the manager said, 'We'll see when we get closer to the day.' The manager didn't let me take the time off, despite my significant amount of overtime."

- "Greg had a dental problem that required an extraction during a work day. He was on medication for pain. The manager asked Greg if the extraction could be done the following day because of the work that needed to be done."

- "I heard a manager ask an employee to schedule her wedding after the 15th of the month so it would not interfere with closing the books."

- "Last night the manager two levels above me had a verbal fit in my office because I was not willing to stay more than half an hour extra. I had my daughter's last soccer game and did not want to miss it. And then he left on time."

- "I was having difficulty with my teenage son; he needed more of my time and attention. When I asked for some latitude in my work schedule, my boss said, 'You need to take care of personal issues on your personal time. That's why God made weekends.'"

- "An employee survey showed a poor response to work/life support for the department, so the manager called a meeting of the entire work group to talk about it . . . on Saturday."

Assess *Your* Situation: Management is insensitive to employees' needs for personal time.	**Frequency: (Circle One)**			
	4 Almost All the Time	**3** Frequently	**2** Occasionally	**1** Almost Never

6. Economic Pressures Create Work Demands

- "I am the controller of a large, privately held family firm. Our management team puts a lot of pressure on employees to work long hours to keep the company competitive. One of my biggest con-

Top Nine Work Inhibitors (*continued*)

cerns is the growing number of people who are out of work in this community and the limited number of job opportunities. Everyone feels that it is better to be overworked than out of work."

- "I chose not to go to my son's championship basketball game. Was it a wrong decision? I don't know. I feel guilty about it. But I have 1500 employees in my organization whom I am responsible for—our business is not doing well, and I need to preserve employment more than attend a basketball game."

- "As a result of the economy, we had a retrenchment [layoff] of 25 percent of the employees, but the work did not go away. Everyone is fearful that he or she will be next, so the extra work we are doing becomes a security blanket. The more we do, the more we feel we will be needed."

- "There is a high stress level in the business. I feel responsible for the results and for the people. It is a source of continuous worry. We have to focus on business results. There used to be pressure to deliver over the year. Now you have to deliver on a quarter-to-quarter basis. You are only as good as your last quarter. The worry takes away concentration from other things, such as the family."

Assess *Your* Situation:	**Frequency: (Circle One)**			
The economy has had a bad impact on our company, and we all have to put in the hours to keep the business operating effectively.	**4** Almost All the Time	**3** Frequently	**2** Occasionally	**1** Almost Never

7. Customers Demand Full and Continual Commitment

- "Years ago my husband suddenly went totally deaf. I became the person who supported the family financially. I have been working for the company for 10 years now. I have a job that requires a high amount of travel, which is difficult with a 5-year-old son. I was on a much-needed vacation with my family when a customer demanded that some changes be made in his job requirements. I came off vacation to help the client. But the client told me it was better if I didn't help—since I could not be 100 percent on the job, I couldn't really help. In the customer's eyes, I had 'failed' because I could not give 100 percent."

- "I've had customers say that my staff were not allowed to go to their university exams because the project work needed to be done."
- "In our business the customer is king. They say 'jump,' and you ask 'how high?' We are at their beck and call every day and all day."

Assess *Your* Situation: The demands I have at work from my customers require me to think about work practically 24 hours a day, 7 days a week.	Frequency: (Circle One)			
	4 Almost All the Time	**3** Frequently	**2** Occasionally	**1** Almost Never

8. Expanding Global Work Demands More Time

- "Our company is trying to expand into more markets outside the country. That means more collaboration with more people in more countries in more time zones. That means more meetings and travel. I can't tell you how many times I have had a conference call at 2 A.M. in order to have my colleagues from Singapore, Belgium, and California on the phone."
- "I work for a U.S.–based international company. Unfortunately, my colleagues in the United States are not very sensitive to time zones. They call meetings that require me to call from home in the late evening and early morning hours. We have a small apartment, so sometimes I just stay at the office rather than disturb my family with a conference call."

Top Nine Work Inhibitors (*continued*)

Assess *Your* Situation:	Frequency: (Circle One)			
Our company has been expanding globally over the last few years, and we end up working prolonged schedules to coordinate and collaborate with our company colleagues around the world.	**4** Almost All the Time	**3** Frequently	**2** Occasionally	**1** Almost Never

9. Company Policies and Technology Encourage More Time at Work

- "One of my children now goes to kindergarten. He thinks I can take Saturday and Sunday off, and he asks why I have to work both days. He asks, 'When can I have fun with my dad?' This has been a real disadvantage of mobile work when you are connected with your work at all times."

- "There was the expectation that when the company started giving work and family benefits, everything else would be okay. We have learned that when the company put in a policy allowing us to work flexibly, a company day-care center, a company cafeteria, or even on-site stores and dry cleaning pick-up, it really just wanted us to be around work more often—to not waste time traveling someplace. The company wants us at work as long as it can entrap us there."

- "Company work/family policies are generally designed to allow a person to work despite having a family—not to allow a person to excel at other priorities besides work."

Assess *Your* Situation:	Frequency: (Circle One)			
The benefits and technology offered by my company encourage us to work longer hours.	**4** Almost All the Time	**3** Frequently	**2** Occasionally	**1** Almost Never

Top Eight Personal and Family Inhibitors

1. Competitive Personality

- "I'm seen as a hard worker, working long hours. People see me get in early (6 A.M.) to begin work. People know that I love my job. I've cut back and have only two or three outside interests. I love my job. Wild horses couldn't keep me away from work. I like to succeed and get results."
- "I'm real focused on time and very driven with regard to results and tasks, and that carries over to my family."
- "Is it my fault for having been driven and caught up in my own work? Did I neglect the children, and have I caused the trouble that's going on? I have two daughters who are divorced, and each of them is having a difficult time as a single parent. I just wonder whether, if I had been a better father, it would have been different or there could have been another outcome for them."

Assess *Your* Situation: I am a competitive person and have a drive to succeed at work, which means my family suffers.	Frequency: (Circle One)			
	4 Almost All the Time	**3** Frequently	**2** Occasionally	**1** Almost Never

2. Impatience with Spouse and Children

- "I have a temper. I am not violent. I just go right to arguing. My children hate to see their mom and dad disagreeing on something, but I am stubborn. That is something I need to work on."
- "I have a bad temper. I kind of do. I have a tendency to solve problems at work constructively, but I don't do the same at home. You're at work and have a hard day with the stresses, and when you get home you unload and let the stresses go."

- "I am used to working with people who follow my directives. When I come home, I am faced with a collection of independent people who frequently don't want to do what I ask them to do. I don't react very patiently to their independence."

Assess *Your* Situation:	**Frequency: (Circle One)**			
I feel impatient with my spouse and my children when they do things in the home differently from how I want them done.	**4** Almost All the Time	**3** Frequently	**2** Occasionally	**1** Almost Never

3. Treating Family Members like Employees

- "When I come home from work, I have a tendency to want to get everything done before I relax, so there's a flurry of activity to get things done, and I probably order my daughter around, telling her to get things picked up or done, when I'm in that mood."
- "In my job I deal with a lot of difficult issues, and then I get criticized by my wife for how I deal with her—'You're not talking to one of your employees.' I tend to be directive."
- "I'm the kind of guy for whom 'sympathy' is found only in the dictionary. I'm not real good at that. It is particularly evident at home."
- "Sometimes we get wrapped up with all the things we have to do in our family, just like at work. I am task-oriented at work and task-oriented at home. We need to do more enjoyable things as a family."

Assess *Your* Situation:	**Frequency: (Circle One)**			
I find that I deal with my family in the same efficient, businesslike way that I deal with people at work.	**4** Almost All the Time	**3** Frequently	**2** Occasionally	**1** Almost Never

4. Family Operates and Makes Decisions Independently

- "I talk every night with my family. But I travel a lot, and when I'm away, they develop their own routines. They make their own decisions. I can become irrelevant—it's tough for me. When you are responsible for 3500 employees, you're used to setting direction and making decisions. It can be frustrating when I come home and their routines are set. I want to go right and they want to go left."
- "I live over 90 miles from the office. My family decided not to move with me closer to work, so I stay close to work for four nights a week and am back home for three nights. They used the rationale that they don't see me much anyway, so it doesn't really matter where we live."
- "We haven't talked about the integration when I am back in the home again. I feel left out of decisions, but they say that I haven't been there to help make decisions. There has to be a specific plan for integrating me back into the family when I get back. I come home on the weekend, and the family has already decided what we're going to do that weekend."

Assess *Your* Situation: My family tends to plan activities and make decisions without first asking my opinion or seeing if I can participate.	**Frequency: (Circle One)**			
	4 Almost All the Time	**3** Frequently	**2** Occasionally	**1** Almost Never

5. Lack of Full Respect for Spouse

- "If I treated people at work the same way I treat my wife, I wouldn't be here at work. They'd fire me."
- "I think I manipulate her. I will lead her down a path to get an answer I want to hear. I may manipulate her to think I am doing more than I'm actually doing around the home—to get more 'points.'"

- "She is interested in my work. I don't bring it home, and I don't talk about it at home. She deserves more than my last 15 minutes of the day, and I don't give much more than that very often."
- "My wife is not feeling that I value and respect what she does in the home or the contribution she makes while I am at work."

Assess *Your* Situation: I am not as respectful as I should be of my spouse's role in the home or at work.	**Frequency: (Circle One)**			
	4 Almost All the Time	**3** Frequently	**2** Occasionally	**1** Almost Never

6. Lack of Listening and Communicating

- "There's no question about it: I get up early in the morning and come home tired. I focus first on the kids, and then I'm so tired that I crash. There is no time to focus on my spouse and very little time to really focus on the children. And my spouse works and does the same thing to me."
- "I don't feel that I am a good friend to my wife the way she thinks I am. You can't be a good friend when you are not listening. I help with the dishes and change diapers, but I don't listen very well."
- "After a hectic day at work, I get absorbed in the paper and TV. I need to put down the paper, turn off the TV, and focus on her and really listen. When I am doing something else, I am not showing that she is important enough for me to listen to her. She is staying home now with the children and is not having a lot of adult conversations during the day."
- "She wants more from me on a daily basis. She will try and stimulate me to talk about people at work, people she knows. But I am tired. I don't want to talk about my work or what is happening at the company."

Top Eight Personal and Family Inhibitors (*continued*)

Assess *Your* Situation:	Frequency: (Circle One)			
I am so occupied by pressures at work that I find it difficult to listen to and communicate with my family.	**4** Almost All the Time	**3** Frequently	**2** Occasionally	**1** Almost Never

7. Impatience with "Trivial" Matters

- "I find that I react to the quality of the conversation. I don't want the details of what happened during the day. That is one of my trigger points when I first get home. My spouse wants to dump a lot of minutiae, details of the day, on me, and I want to romp on the floor with the kids. I asked my spouse to give me a few minutes to 'detox,' to wind down from the day, before listening to what happened during the day."

- "At the end of the day, I don't want to hear all the things that were irritating during the day. I have enough to think about from work, and I really don't want to hear all the small problems that occurred."

Assess *Your* Situation:	Frequency: (Circle One)			
I feel impatient with my family when I come home and they want to talk about trivial things.	**4** Almost All the Time	**3** Frequently	**2** Occasionally	**1** Almost Never

8. Lack of Interest in Children's Activities and Hobbies

- "Our 5-year-old gets left out sometimes. I don't think he is getting a fair shake, compared to the others. I take my 10-year-old to play golf, but the 5-year-old is left out of it. I need to do things together with the two of them and then also do things with them individually."

> • "My children are into Yugio cards. I have a hard time being supportive of their hobby. I am not really openly critical, but I don't make a lot of time for it. My child will make his own Yugio card on a paper and give it to me, but I don't respond."

Assess *Your* Situation:	Frequency: (Circle One)			
I usually enjoy sharing activities and hobbies with my children only if they are doing something that I am interested in.	**4** Almost All the Time	**3** Frequently	**2** Occasionally	**1** Almost Never

EXERCISE: *Identify and Quantify Your Inhibitors*

In order to achieve our desired future state, to end up where we want to be with our personal relationships, we need to understand what may be working against us. We need to understand what may inhibit our achieving our goals. Then we need to identify ways in which we can control or influence those inhibitors. We need to work on influencing the inhibitors as much as or more than they influence us. Even some slight changes in our behavior can result in work inhibitors and personal and family inhibitors losing some of the stranglehold they may have over our lives.

In order to assess the pressures you feel from your work and family and to determine which area most of the pressures come from, calculate the number of inhibitors in the following way:

- Add up the number of situations in which you experience work contributor pressure "almost all the time," "frequently," "occasionally," or "almost never." Write the number of each in the space provided.
- Multiply by the numerical values 4 through 1 and place the score in the blank space.
- Add up the total of the numbers in the four boxes and place the number in the right column box. This becomes your baseline number for your work inhibitors. The overall number will be helpful for tracking

and measuring your progress over time and for assessing where you may have an opportunity to make a change.

- Repeat this procedure for personal and family inhibitors.

	How many situations had an Almost All the Time or 4 response?	How many situations had a Frequently or 3 response?	How many situations had an Occasionally or 2 response?	How many situations had an Almost Never or 1 response?	Add up the numbers in the four columns to get a total number
Work inhibitors	_____ of responses x 4 = _____	_____ of responses x 3 = _____	_____ of responses x 2 = _____	_____ of responses x 1 = _____	Total:
Personal and family inhibitors	_____ # of responses x 4 = _____	_____ # of responses x 3 = _____	_____ # of responses x 2 = _____	_____ # of responses x 1 = _____	Total:

What We Control and What We Don't

Look at the final figures you have written down and ask yourself the following questions:

- Do you have higher scores from the work inhibitors or from the personal and family inhibitors?
- Are there more 4 and 3 responses than 2 and 1 responses?
- Do you have a total score of more than 22.5 on the work inhibitors?
- Do you have a total score of more than 20 on the personal and family inhibitors?

Let's look at some of the ways in which we can control our situation and then return to our scores to identify some ways to lower the total scores for the work inhibitors and for the personal and family inhibitors.

In order to reprogram our thinking, we need to understand what we truly control and what we don't control. When we coach someone through the process of improving her or his personal relationships, we emphasize the need to first work on "self." If we try to improve our own attitude and personal functioning in the family, we will have a much better chance at resolving some of the fundamental problems that exist *outside* of our own personal control. In other words, if we can seek first to understand ourself, then we will be far more likely to be able to influence those around us. Others will be far more open to our influence. They will see our sincere efforts to improve and repair damaged relationships, and often they will make similar efforts.

For example:

- One cause of a deteriorating relationship with your spouse may be the way your spouse tries to solve problems. Perhaps he is forceful and demanding in getting his solution accepted. That is outside of your control. What you do have control over, however, is the approach you take to address his forceful, one-sided method of problem-solving. How do you respond? You do have control over your impatience and anger, and over how you address the situation.

- Your boss may be very demanding of your time. He asks you to work overtime, sometimes in direct conflict with your personal plans. Your hours may be long. You may feel squeezed between your longing to be with your family and your need to provide for your family. Much of the situation is outside of your control. But you do have control over how you respond to your boss, how you try to prevent workload crises, how you deliver results, and how you spend the sliver of time that you have left for your family.

- Perhaps your teenage children ignore you, would never think of being seen with you at the mall, and generally don't like to engage in any conversation with you other than mumbling "fine" to your inquiry about them. Much of this is normal teenage behavior, which every parent experiences to some extent. You don't have control over your children's behavior. But you do have control over how you approach them, how you respond to them when they ignore you, and how you begin to repair and rebuild your relationship with them.

As we realize we have some degree of control over our situation, we can better be able to confront and handle work pressure and self-pressure.

Work Pressure

In today's competitive work environment, longer hours seems to be a permanent part of work. A grandfather described the evolution he has experienced as a farmer:

> When I purchased my first tractor, I could work from sunup to sundown when the weather was nice. When the sun went down, I knew it was time to go in. Then they put cabs on the tractors, so we could work and be productive in all types of weather, hot or cold, rain or sunshine. We could even work through our lunch and breaks. But darn it all, then they put headlights on them tractors!

Compounding the challenge of working longer hours is the commonly accepted view of work hours as a measure of performance. Employees often work long hours under the mistaken belief that hours worked are a measure of their productivity. Managers use work hours as a currency, often using them in place of good performance and frequently tipping the scales in favor of promotions and rewards for the employees who put in the most hours.

In addition, many erroneous beliefs and assumptions have permeated the work environment, reinforced by insensitive managers and capitulating employees alike. Here are the typical roadblocks that employees have told us they experience in their companies:

- Ambition to succeed at work and ambition to succeed in interests and activities outside of work are incompatible.
- Career development is a sink-or-swim model. If you stop your career progression (historically defined as upward movement) to achieve balance outside of work, you eliminate future progress.
- The total hours worked equals the contribution to the organization.
- Personal problems are a nonbusiness issue.
- Flexibility on work and family issues is discouraged because it will only lead to a feeling of entitlement.

- "We pay you well, so you should solve your own problems."
- "You have to pay your dues; we all did."
- Work and family balance is a women's issue.

Ironically, work and personal life can be compatible and complementary. As the president of a large division at a top U.S. company said,

> Work and personal life complement one another. When there are problems at work, there is a spillover to the home, and when there are problems with the home, there is a spillover to the work. *But, both work and family should be able to enrich each other—a person should be enriched by both experiences.* There should be an equilibrium.

Dr. Peter Senge from MIT emphasizes that corporations can no longer ignore the connection between work and personal life. By not treating employees in a holistic way, they ignore the very source of the values that employees bring to the company; they exploit the employee without regard to the source of his or her qualities and characteristics. A company that relies on the personal growth of employees for its continual growth and renewal needs to support "personal mastery in all aspects of life."

> It cannot foster shared vision without calling forth personal visions, and personal visions are always multifaceted—they always include deeply felt desires for our personal, professional, organization, and family lives.

Dr. Senge further suggests that we have created an "artificial boundary between work and family" that runs counter to running the company as a complete and holistic system. He concludes that work and family are linked and can provide synergy to each other. After all, "one cannot build [an effective] organization on a foundation of broken homes and strained personal relationships."

Remember Robert from the first chapter? Here is his description of how he handles some work situations in order to exert more control.

> I made some rules for myself that included saving the weekends for the family, attending important family occasions and scheduling family vacations. The first time I spoke with my boss about my rules, I got chal-

lenged at work. (This was when I was in a lower position.) The boss came looking for me at 7 A.M. I told him in a nice way, "My life is my life. Judge me by what I get done." I proceeded to describe what I wanted to do to achieve my work objectives, but not at the expense of my family. The boss was not pleased at first, but then said, "You're right." Now I live by my rules. I'm in control to a greater extent.

I had made the decision as to what my rules are. I didn't know what my boss would say. My original boss was shocked. Some people say that family is important, but don't act on it and then blame the company— the company is not always at fault.

Self-Pressure

Everyone feels the reality of the pressures at work. Unfortunately, many of us get sucked into the "success spiral." This is the phenomenon, described by Dr. Senge, in which work success reinforces more investment in work. Nagging pressures to remain successful at work encourage more investment in work, which leads to more success at work. Less time at home may lead to poorer family relationships, which, in turn, reinforce the need to avoid being at home too long. There is a continual spiral that holds the willing participants captive as they continue to gravitate to the place where they feel most rewarded and away from the area where they feel the least amount of reward.

Realize Your Power of Choice

There are a variety of reasons why family relationships are not what they should be. Some of them are very real; others are perceived by our minds as factors over which we have no control, but in reality are self-imposed. Too often we are faced with dilemmas about family relationships and assume that we have no control over the situation. This is almost to say that for every stimulus, we have a set response.

We always have choice. For every contributor that causes family relationships to suffer, we have choice in how we respond to that stimulus. We can decide how we want to respond. Many people have told us that they have no control over how they respond to a situation that may hurt family relationships. In fact, we always have choice.

- One executive explained to us that early in his career he had worked for a rather intimidating and abusive boss. This boss would constantly test the allegiance of his group by seeing if his direct reports would do what he asked them to do: attend meetings on the weekend, work very late on projects that did not require late hours, and so on. He was very controlling and manipulative. On one occasion, he called a late-night staff meeting on Halloween night. Everyone was very upset about the meeting, particularly those who had planned to go trick-or-treating with their children. Most were so intimidated by the boss that they decided to be at the staff meeting rather than be with their families. However, one member of the team would not let the stimulus of a bad boss calling a staff meeting on an important family night dictate the response that everyone else felt was the only possible solution. She went to the boss for a private meeting. She was clear with the boss that she was supportive and loyal to him, but that her family took top priority. She said that she would work late any other night or do whatever was required, but that Halloween night was reserved for her family. To her surprise, the boss backed down, said that he admired someone who would take a stand for her family, and excused her from attending the meeting. Her peers all attended the Halloween night staff meeting. The employee who took a stand had a different relationship with her boss from that time forward. She was not pushed around but was actually respected by her boss.

- A work group was advised that its workload would increase by over 50 percent in the coming year without any increase in head count. The group already ran a 24-hour, 7-days-a-week operation, so it decided to pool its resources and knowledge to figure out how to work more efficiently. Together, led by one employee who took charge, the group trimmed back on work process, cross-trained employees in order to have more employees capable of providing back-up, and outsourced some work to vendors. In addition, it arranged work schedules into four 10-hour days, which provided everyone with more flexibility and actually eliminated the time required to transition or "hand-off work" between shifts.

- Another executive was unhappy with his life but felt pressure to stay in his job. He had a senior-level position with a large corporation. He made plenty of money, but he wasn't spending the time he wanted with his family. One day he asked his wife where she would live and sink down roots for the family if she had a choice. They loved the mountains, and they decided that the place would be Colorado. He told her to take their oldest daughter and fly out to Colorado for the weekend. He said that if they could find a place in Colorado where they wanted to live, he would notify his management that he would be leaving the company. They took him at his word, found a wonderful home for the family, and returned home. On Monday he went and told his boss that he was leaving the company and moving to Colorado. He did not have a job lined up; he had just decided to make a change in his life. Most of his peers thought he was crazy to just up and quit without having another job. They thought he was crazy to leave a job in a premier company with a big title and comfortable money. His response was consistent and honest: "I did it for the sake of my family." Despite all the trappings of success, he realized that he had choice, and he decided to exercise it regardless of what others thought.

- Another senior level professional was very successful at her job. She was also a single mother. Whenever she came home from work to her two children, she continued the script she did so well at the office. She pushed and drove the children to do their homework and chores. Her children pushed back, did not cooperate, and tried to avoid being home when she first arrived. Communication was tense, tempers flared easily, and criticism was frequent. A major relationship barrier emerged that tended to drive the children to their friends and out of the home. She decided she could not control their behavior and feelings, but she could control hers. She loosened up in her post-work repertoire, played with the children, and asked about their day. It took some time, but the children began seeing the fun mother they once knew. Soon they started to participate in solving problems around the house—when the chores were to be done, when homework should be done, what their rewards would be, and when they would go on special family outings. It wasn't a perfect situation, but she changed the situation by choosing to work on herself.

EXERCISE: *Identifying Targets for Improving Your Control*

Now, let's see if we can lower your scores for work inhibitors and personal and family inhibitors. The purpose of this exercise is to identify and focus on two or three of the inhibitors for which you can drop the score by one number. Return to your list. Of those inhibitors for which you have a score of 3 or 4, which ones could you lower by one number (e.g., from a 4 down to a 3, or from a 3 down to a 2)?

- Write the specific inhibitors with a 4 score in the space provided in the second column of the following table.
- Write the specific inhibitors with a 3 score in the space provided in the third column.
- Over which of the work inhibitors do you feel you could really have influence or exert more control? For which work inhibitors could you drop the score by one number? Write your response in the column on the right.
- Over which of the personal and family inhibitors do you really feel you could have influence or exert more control? For which personal and family inhibitors could you drop the score by one number? Write your response in the column on the right.

Try to identify enough inhibitors to lower your score to 22.5 or less for the work inhibitor section and to 20 or less for the personal and family inhibitor section.

Next, identify the specific actions you could take that would lead each inhibitor to drop by at least one number:

- Write your proposed action in the space provided in the Specific Action Plan on page 54.
- Review your proposed actions with your spouse and family to gain their input into your plan. You should use your family as "consultants" to comment on your plans even if your actions focus on work inhibitors about which you feel your family has little knowledge and over which it has little influence.

	How many situations had an Almost All the Time or 4 response?	How many situations had a Frequently or 3 response?	
Work inhibitors	Number of responses with a 4 rating: _____	Number of responses with a 3 rating: _____	
List the specific work inhibitors with a rating of 4 or 3	• • • • •	• • • • •	Identify two work inhibitors that you feel you could improve by one rating (e.g., from a 4 to a 3 or from a 3 to a 2): 1. 2.

We have worked with many people who believe that they have no choice but to stay in a job or advance to a position in which they are not happy. Both actions can have a negative impact on the family. We are not suggesting that everyone quit her or his job and move to the land of her or his choice. We do, however, believe that *we have far more choice in what we do, how we do it, and when we do it than we realize.*

	How many situations had an Almost All the Time or 4 response?	**How many situations had a Frequently or 3 response?**	
Personal and family inhibitors	Number of responses with a 4 rating: _____	Number of responses with a 3 rating: _____	
List the specific personal and family inhibitors with a rating of 4 or 3	• • • • •	• • • • •	Identify two personal and family inhibitors that you feel you could improve by one rating (e.g., from a 4 to a 3 or from a 3 to a 2) 1. 2.

Specific Action Plan

What actions could you take to influence and improve your control over the work and family inhibitors? Select only two or three actions that you will take to influence and control the work and family inhibitors:

1.

2.

3.

4.

5.

We have also worked with many people who believe that they don't have the option to improve their personal relationships. Either they feel *they* can't change (e.g., "That's just the way I am. I've developed the habit of being impatient. I can't change."), or they feel that *their family members* will not change (e.g., "My daughter doesn't listen to me anymore. She is disobedient. I get impatient with her. She shuts me out. The cycle repeats itself continuously.") We also believe we have more choice in shaping our moods, thinking, and behavior—in what we do and how we respond to our family—than we realize.

The challenge is to identify one or two areas to influence, either in our work or in our family, and to work to improve and control the situation a little at a time.

In summary, we have been discussing how to close the gap between where we are and where we want to be by assessing and changing our patterns of thinking. We described the need to (1) rebalance our definition of success to include personal and family relations and (2) reprogram our power of choice by recognizing the degree of control we actually have over our situation despite the many work and family inhibitors we face each day. Changing our thinking is an important first step toward resetting our direction.

As important as it is for us to rethink our situation, capturing our thinking in a written document to describe our relationship goals is far more powerful. We will complete this thinking process in Chapter 5 by walking through an exercise we use in our coaching to establish a written personal "family legacy." This family legacy is a way to establish a target for where we want to go with our relationships and how we want to be remembered.

CHAPTER 4

Behave Your Way into a New Way of Thinking

"It's easier to behave your way into a new way of thinking, than to think your way into a new way of behaving."

—Anonymous

IN THIS CHAPTER we want to describe how behavior will transform our thinking into new, effective personal behavior through three important principles or behavioral success factors:

- Law of the harvest
- Law of increasing returns
- The power of being influenced and of apologizing

These three behavioral success factors, combined with reprogramming our thinking, can help to clear out the fog that prevents us from reaching our desired end state.

The behavioral success factors focus on our behavior toward the people with whom we have close personal relationships. *Effective personal relationships have almost nothing to do with skills and training; they have almost everything to do*

57

with consistent and unrelenting love. These three success factors are the ultimate expression of love, not the outcome of graduating from a human relations class. If they are integrated and programmed into our behavior, these success factors can make the difference between having successful, meaningful relationships and having lukewarm, struggling relationships.

It is difficult to change behavior. It is difficult to change deeply ingrained patterns of thinking and ways of responding to situations. However, we can change, and these behavioral success factors are vital if we are to behave in a different and more effective way within our relationships. More important, these behavioral success factors actually help to accelerate our thinking process. We have found that changing our way of thinking helps to establish a direction, but changing our behavior helps to accelerate our personal commitment to following our thinking and getting to our final desired destination. Our thinking influences our behavior, and our behavior, in turn, influences our thinking.

The adage "it is easier to behave your way into a new way of thinking than to think your way into a new way of behaving" has great merit in personal relationships. If we can behave in a prescribed way, we will soon find that we have changed our head and our heart. If we learn to drive a stick shift, we will eventually have the movements programmed into our head so that we carry them out automatically. If we serve others, we will eventually love to serve. If we sacrifice our time and effort for someone we love, we will grow in our love for that person. If we can begin to behave in more constructive, helpful ways, we will solidify our commitment to the direction in which we want to go. Ultimately, it becomes easier to change ingrained behavior.

In the field of physics, there are two forms of energy, one of which is called *potential energy* and the other *kinetic energy*. Potential energy is energy at rest, energy that an object possesses by virtue of its location (e.g., a dam and the water behind it, a car on a hill with the parking brake on, a rock perched on the edge of a cliff). Kinetic energy is the energy of a body in motion (e.g., the water flowing out from behind the dam, a car driving down the street, a rock falling from a cliff). Thinking about behaving differently is good, like potential energy, but it is not nearly as powerful as acting differently, based on our thinking. If we store in our head ideas about how we can be a better person, but we do not act on our knowledge, we have "potential energy" but not the energy to make a real difference. It is our kinetic energy, acting on our ideas and becoming the person we want to become, that releases our true potential and drives us toward our future state.

Behavioral Fog

As we coach individuals on how to close the gap, reach their desired future state, and achieve their ultimate level of personal relationships, we find that there are three factors that blind individuals and prevent them from achieving their goal of improving relationships. We call these factors *behavioral fog*. The fog consists of (1) seeking instant gratification, (2) following the law of diminishing returns, and (3) buying our own set of the emperor's new clothes by deluding ourself as to our infallibility.

These "fog" factors are habits of behavior that obscure our future state and slow down our progress toward it. They are behaviors that we have consistently engaged in over a period of time, so they have become programmed into our behavioral repertoire. If we get lost in this behavioral fog, we will become discouraged and lose direction, and eventually our progress may come to a stop. At best, these behavioral fog factors will slow our progress toward our goal (provided we are following a clearly delineated and marked path). But at worst, these behavioral fog factors can turn us completely around and head us in the wrong direction without our even knowing that we are headed in the wrong direction. Individuals who recognize that they are experiencing behavioral fog and who clear out the fog from their habits of behavior and replace it with some new behaviors can see their direction more clearly and even *accelerate* their movement toward their final destination. They are more likely to close the gap between their current state and their future state quickly.

There are three critical behavioral success factors that form a powerful entry point for changing our behavior. We will first discuss the behavioral fog and then show how the three behavioral success factors can be a beacon of light that will guide us through the fog.

Common Behavioral Fog Factors

1. Instant Gratification

Beginning in our youth and continuing throughout our life, we learn to expect instant results. We buy instant chocolate milk, ready-to-eat dinners, and frozen vegetables. We work hard because we know we will be paid in a week or two. We want to receive a high salary just out of school, we want to become CEO by the age of 35, and we want a top-of-the-line car and our dream house now. At work we drive for improvements in daily revenue and quarterly profits. We invest in the stock market and expect our portfolio to increase in value within the quarter, or we grow concerned. Some have described us as the "we want it now" generation.

One need only look at the amount of debt that people have assumed as a percentage of their income to recognize how much the buy-now–pay-later mentality has permeated our society.

In many circles, delayed gratification (the opposite of instant gratification) is not seen as a virtue; rather, it is seen as the antithesis of being driven, goal-oriented, and achieving. We reward and encourage driven individuals who get results quickly. We watch TV shows that present a perplexing problem and play on our emotions for 59 minutes, then provide the solution to the problem or the resolution of the situation in a neat, tidy package before the final commercials. We eulogize leaders who are decisive and who get results quickly. We want a war with Iraq won in 20 days with fewer than 100 casualties. We applaud the captains of industry who drive their corporations to enhance their quarterly earnings and our stock portfolio at the same time. We want to see our dividends grow, and if they don't, we question the leadership of the corporation.

On the other hand, individuals who delay gratification and have a long-term focus may not earn our respect. Perhaps they spent a significant amount of time in building consensus or collaborating with others. They may, in fact, be characterized as "indecisive," "undriven," or "not leadership material." We may have the erroneous belief that they are not "results-oriented" or they lack initiative. We can't imagine Superman walking to the scene of a crime, John Wayne trying to patiently talk his way out of a tough situation, or Keanu Reeves from *The Matrix* being so slow that he is hit by a bullet.

2. The Law of Diminishing Returns

In business we are familiar with the law of diminishing returns. The law states that we achieve an optimal result after an investment of a certain amount of time, energy, and money. The result reaches a peak, after which the investment of additional time, energy, and money no longer pays off as well as before. At that point, we pull back our effort in order to preserve our capital and energy. For example, we may spend 3 hours writing a report or preparing a presentation. We may then spend another 3 hours going over it and refining the wording and the presentation of the material. But few of us would take another 3 hours to go over it yet again and further fine-tune the material. Why? Our minor changes in the presentation would not be worth the investment of our energy and time. We understand the law of diminishing returns.

In the home, we may apply a coat of paint to a room and then a second coat of paint, and perhaps a third. But at some point we feel that the end result will not be better with further investment of time and energy and the cost of the paint. We believe in conservation of energy. So we stop. We believe in and expect early results, with only just enough personal investment. If the results don't come, we pull back on our investment.

In our family and personal relationships, if we have a son who constantly rebels against our wishes or a daughter who seems determined not to follow our counsel, we grow weary. We leave correction and discipline to the other spouse. We pick our battles and weigh in only on important matters. If we are faced with a constant barrage of negative and confrontational interactions in our family, we may eventually cease our interactions altogether and stop giving our family members the kind of love they need. If we are constantly bickering in a marriage, the soured relationship eventually no longer seems worth the investment of emotional energy, and we may withdraw from the relationship or seek a separation. A marriage may cease to have the spark it had in its early days and degenerate into a relationship of convenience. Relationships with children may arrive at a point where their departure is both anticipated and welcome. We often adhere to the law of diminishing returns in our relationships and expend only so much energy before we grow weary of our efforts and feel that we no longer benefit from the investment.

The law of diminishing returns is different from instant gratification. Our tendency toward instant gratification leads us to expect immediate results from our efforts. Instant gratification is a stimulus-response behavior; we do something, and we expect something in return. With our tendency to follow the law of diminishing returns, we recognize that energy and effort and investment are needed, perhaps over a period of time . . . *but only to the extent that we are benefited in return.* We may realize that our personal and family relationships need our time and effort, but we provide that time and effort only to the extent that we feel we are rewarded for doing so. If we feel that we are wasting our time, we minimize our physical and emotional investment and back off from being a fully engaged spouse or parent. Or we expend effort over a period of time, become discouraged at the results, and withdraw our effort altogether.

3. The Delusion of Infallibility: The Emperor's New Clothes

We are all familiar with the story "The Emperor's New Clothes." Two charlatans decide to appeal to the emperor's vanity by making him some clothes with exclusive, invisible thread. They pretend to make these fabulous clothes for the emperor, but in reality they have not made any clothes. The emperor, unable to recognize when he is wrong, puts on the "invisible clothes" and then parades through the streets stark naked. No one wants to tell the emperor the truth—that he has no clothes on. In his own vanity and self-infatuation, he goes along with the charlatans until a small, innocent child says out loud, "The emperor doesn't have any clothes on!" and the truth emerges.

We have worked with very exceptional people—driven, achievement-oriented people who have done well at their chosen occupation and have been successful throughout their life. Their entire history is one of exercising good judgment and being right more often than they have been wrong—that is why they have been promoted and rewarded. As a result of their successful track record, they tend to get used to being right most of the time and may frequently act as if they are always right (or at least rarely wrong). They rely on their own judgment and trust in that judgment and their capabilities—after all, history has proven them right. Like most of us, they tend to want to appear competent and in command of the situation and are reluctant to show any vulnerability or weakness. In corporations, they tend to rise to a level where people around them are uncomfortable giving them hard and critical feedback. They become the emperor of our story.

But in fact, these driven people can and do make errors; they are wrong at times. For some of them, the hardest thing to do is to recognize they are wrong and then to apologize. They feel that an apology will somehow diminish their self-esteem, acknowledge a deficiency in their behavior, or make them subservient to the person to whom they have apologized. Plus, it just feels uncomfortable—no one likes to "eat humble pie."

We find a chain of events in the lives of individuals who wear the emperor's clothes. They experience three diseases of "the heart" in varying degrees of intensity that erode their judgment over time:

1. *Pride of heart.* They have an exaggerated sense of their own accomplishments and superiority. They measure people against a higher, unrealistic yardstick and find almost everyone coming up short. A solution is good to the extent that they had input into that solution. They are not easily influenced or persuaded by others whose views differ from their own.

2. *Hardness of heart.* They tend to be insensitive to the feelings of others, being unduly critical and callous in their approach to dealing with problems. They can be unforgiving of others who do not meet their standards or who deviate from what they consider to be the norm. They have clear ideas of what is right and what is wrong. They establish rules in the home that are based on their own good judgment, and they have little tolerance for someone, such as an independent teenager in the family, who does not follow these rules. They can seem uncaring and harsh at times.

3. *Idleness of heart.* As a result of their pride and their hardness, they tend not to engage actively in the real work of building and maintaining strong relationships. *In essence, they are blind to the first two diseases— pride of heart and hardness of heart—and see no need to change anything in their own behavior.* Their approach has made them successful at work, and they believe that the same approach will make them successful in personal and family relationships. They expect others to take the initiative—after all, they feel that others have flaws in their character. They lack prolonged effort and are slothful in healing a stagnating relationship.

So how do these three diseases of the heart manifest themselves in busy people? First, these people tend to be impatient and are often quick to get angry, particularly with members of their family. The lowest score on the Family 360 instrument has been on the question "Solves problems without getting angry." On a scale of 1 to 7, with 7 being the most favorable, the executives we have coached rate themselves an average of 3.4. Their spouses gave the executives an average score of 4.2, and their children gave their executive father or mother an average score of 4.1. The executives' low self-score indicates that they are well aware of this flaw. When we work with these individuals, we find that they are quick to become impatient and slow to admit they are wrong. Some become angry easily and raise their voice with little provocation. Their impatience and anger can serve to create a wedge within their personal relationships. As was the case with the emperor who had no clothes on, their anger can make others hesitant to tell them the real truth; no one likes to be on the receiving end of an angry tirade. Clearly, anger was the most problematic characteristic of the executive group.

Second, these people tend not to apologize, nor to admit their error. They continue in their self-delusion. This form of fog prevents them from seeing the need to behave differently, since they believe that the problem does not rest with them. They see the problem as residing in others. Again, the data from the Family 360 survey shed some light on this issue.

Normally, individuals tend to rate themselves more critically on the Family 360 survey instrument than their spouse and their children rate them.

They usually recognize when they have a tendency to behave in a wrong way. For example, they recognized their anger to a greater degree than their spouse or children did. Interestingly, however, there were 2 questions out of the total of 58 on which the participants scored themselves on average higher than their spouse scored them. Thus, there were two areas where the participants felt that they were doing better than their spouse felt they were doing—two areas where they may not have recognized a flaw in their behavior as clearly as their spouse did. One of these survey questions is, "Apologizes when he/she has done something wrong." The other is, "Forgives past mistakes of individual family members." The participants felt that they were better at apologizing and forgiving others, on average, than others felt they were.

Not only are apologizing and forgiving two behaviors that are hard for us to do, but, as the survey indicates, we often do not recognize the need to do so. Like the emperor, we don't recognize when we are wrong, so we don't seek to apologize. Or, we fault others for not meeting our exacting standard of performance and are not magnanimous enough to forgive them for their shortcomings. Our delusion of infallibility is a major area of behavioral fog because we may not even recognize when we are wrong or headed in the wrong direction.

Clearing Behavioral Fog: Three Behavioral Success Factors

These three forms of behavioral fog can distort reality in two ways:

1. They can obscure the direction in which we are going and put us on a trajectory that will not lead to where we really want to go.
2. More important, these types of behavioral fog can obscure the *need* to do anything differently. We may not even realize that we are heading in the wrong direction—in fact, we may feel that we are perfectly on track.

However, there are three behavioral principles that directly confront and address the behavioral fog.

1. The Law of the Harvest

We understand the "law of the harvest" because it is a natural law that many of us have experienced firsthand. We reap what we sow. We harvest what we tend and grow. In farming, some crops require only a short period of time to germinate, grow, and bear fruit. Some crops spring up and can be harvested early in the summer; others grow for a late harvest. Still others may take months or years. Asparagus and rhubarb, for example, produce their first full harvestable crop only in the second year of growth. Berries and fruit trees require careful nurturing, fertilizing, cross-pollination, and care for years before they yield a significant harvest. Slow-growing crops are not for the impatient farmer.

The law of the harvest is a natural law that runs counter to the fog of instant gratification. It applies both at work and in our homes. At work, we invest effort and expect a paycheck. We accomplish goals and expect a harvest of rewards. In our families, we raise and nurture children; we develop personal relationships and love. Some relationships must be nurtured for years in order to mature and grow. But we see gradual growth, and we know that progress is being made.

Some relationships take time to develop, and some take time to heal after years of neglect. It can be difficult to wait for some of our important relationships to grow and bear fruit. We want our relationships to be perfect now. We want our children to be successful and happy and well mannered now, not in the future. Families need our best nurturing and caretaking over a long period of time. Investment in the family does not necessarily provide immediate gratification.

What does this mean for us? How do we need to behave differently? We need to keep in check our impulse to want instant results with our family. Within our family relationships, we need to act in ways that provide our family members with choice and with age-appropriate independence and control.

2. The Law of Increasing Returns

Jim and Ellen are the parents of seven children and grandparents to sixteen children. Jim described his long-term relationships with his children:

We raised our children to the best of our ability, but several of the children took off in directions we did not like. I was very familiar with our local police. Most of our children had a variety of problems and habits, including drinking and smoking marijuana.

But, neither Jim nor his wife gave up on their children, even when they eventually left home to struggle on their own. They maintained their ties as a family and continued some of their traditions when they gathered as a family. Their favorite tradition was to make cookies as a family in the shapes of family members and friends. This tradition had started 30 years earlier when some of the first teenagers in the family made cookies in the shape of their boy- and girlfriends."

Six years ago, when all of the children were married and out of the home, tragedy struck the family. One of the youngest daughters, a young woman 32 years of age with three children, died of a drug overdose. Jim recalls, "It sent an electric shock of grief through the entire family. But it also sent a wake-up call to the children. Most of them stopped their heavy drinking and drug use." Jim, then over 60 years old and still working, stopped all his international trips and stayed close to home for the next year. He spent even more time with his children and grandchildren. "You can't just dry up and blow away as a father or grandfather, or become a retired, rocking chair-bound parent in the 'elephant's graveyard' of retirees."

Some of his children were struggling financially, so he helped them learn how to budget and raise a family on limited resources, skills that he had acquired years earlier. He pulled the family together to talk about their sister and his daughter and how much she meant to them. They continued their tradition of cookie making. Most notably, Jim and his wife traveled across the country to their daughter in Arizona. She and her family were struggling to make ends meet. As a family, they agreed to have the daughter, her husband, and their children move back into Jim's home in the East. Jim and his wife worked with their son-in-law to get him qualified and ready to find a better job. Jim used some of his contacts to land his son-in-law job interviews. After 6 months in their home, the son-in-law was offered a promising position in a large company in the area. The family became stable again, and they moved into their own home.

Jim and his wife took a long-term perspective on the family relationship. Despite the challenges and problems their children posed for them as parents, they continued to try to strengthen and renew their relationships long after the children had left home. In Jim's words, "You need to create a feeling that they can always come home, because you love them no matter what."

How difficult it is to wait when we get so little in return! When we expect to have an immediate return on our investment (instant gratification) *or* when we follow the law of diminishing returns and back off on our effort too soon when results don't come quickly, we head toward disappointment in our relationships. Nowhere is this more true than in our personal and family relationships. As Jim and his wife came to understand, relationships take time to develop and grow, sometimes over a lifetime. If we expect immediate success in our personal relationships or, worse, if we stop trying when our personal relationships momentarily stagnate, then we will ultimately not have the rich and lasting relationships that we seek. Some of our richest associations may even occur when we are grandparents.

Our first attempts to mend a relationship may be unsuccessful. Even our second attempts, our third attempts, or later attempts may not succeed. Dr. Henry B. Eyring, a well-known educator, described the law of increasing returns and noted that at work our paycheck comes often, but in the family our "paycheck" may come only a few times in a lifetime. It takes continual, constant, unrelenting effort to build and grow personal relationships. A close examination of our own relationships would help assess our adherence to the law:

- Are we willing to sacrifice our time and energy, our heart and soul, when we receive little in return?
- How can we keep patiently watching and waiting when we don't see results in our relationships?
- Are we willing to persist in strengthening our relationships with our children after years of rebellious behavior and long after they have left the home?
- Will we overlook years of criticism from our spouse and take active steps to mend the relationship?

- Will we reach out to a relative or close family member who has offended us in the past and doesn't seem open to repairing the relationship with us?

The law of increasing returns is our commitment to spending time to build the relationship even when we don't see incremental progress. One CEO we met with expressed how difficult it is to build and maintain good personal and family relationships:

> The greatest lesson I've learned is that personal and family relationships take as much work as your work life. If you think you can neglect them and still do a good job at them, you're wrong, and you'll destroy them just like you'll destroy anything else. I think a lot people who graduate from college and get a job don't realize how hard they're going to work. They're ambitious, and they think that they don't have to focus on family, that this stuff will take care of itself—both your personal relationships and your relationship with your kids. Ambitious people think that quality time with your kids will make up for quantity. That's just not true; it is a falsity. *You have to have a certain amount of quantity to get the quality.*

Implementing the law of increasing returns involves *putting in a quantity of time and effort over a long period of time.* It means playing the "bo-bo doll," being willing to be punched down and coming back up each time. Jim and Ellen did not give up, even when their children broke all the rules of their home. This is not a Pollyannaish approach to life. The law of increasing returns is a continuation of the law of the harvest. It recognizes that between harvests we have to fertilize, till the earth, and prepare the ground. We have to keep the farm equipment running and in good order. We have to repair the roof, mend the fence, and feed the chickens. We have to invest in our property and equipment. And if we are patient, in the fourth or seventh or fifteenth season of our work, we will realize a harvest that we can feel good about.

As parents, we need to invest in our relationships with putting in a quantity of time and effort over a long period of time. We need to maintain our personal and family relationships when the behavior of our children is embarrassing to us, contrary to our values, or contrary to how we have taught them. We need to keep the bonds strong both when children are home and when they are out of the home and gone. And, if we are patient, in the fourth or seventh or fifteenth year of our work, or even when we are grandparents, we will break even or realize some gain that makes the effort worthwhile.

3. The Power of Being Influenced and of Apologizing

Our own delusion of infallibility can be quickly swept away in the face of a challenging interpersonal relationship: a rebellious teenager, critical in-laws, a spouse with strong and differing views. We realize that while we may see ourselves as infallible, others do not see us this way. And, unlike in our work, we may not be in a position of authority over the situation. It is at these very moments that we are put to the test and we find out how helpful it is to be open to being influenced, to accepting criticism, and to understanding differing perspectives.

The power of being influenced is well illustrated by the example of Juergen and Mei-Li. They are in one of the most challenging personal relationships, an interracial marriage. Juergen is German, and Mei-Li is Chinese.

> Few people realize how difficult it is to be married when there are so many dividers right from the start. We met in Germany. Mei-Li was fluent in English and spoke some German, so we were able to communicate. But marriage brought out the many differences we have: We like different food: She likes spicy Asian food, and I like traditional German food. She likes noodles; I like bread and cheese. She comes from a strict Asian upbringing; I come from a relaxed and open European family. We have different family traditions and celebrate different holidays. My parents are from a financially secure background and live in a beautiful home; her parents are poor farmers who live in a small shanty with no heating. She believes we should raise our children one way; I believe there is a better way to raise them. Surprisingly, we have a common set of religious values that set the foundation for a good relationship.

I realized early in our relationship, about the time our daughter was born, that there were certain things I had to do to preserve and strengthen our relationship. I needed to become open to trying new things, eating new foods, learning a new language. I backed off from my stance on German food. It's okay that if I want some German food, I have to make it myself or go to my mother's for her delicious Rulladen. Along with backing off, I had to adopt new practices. I adopted many of her holidays, traditions, and practices. I realized early that our relationship was more important than a tradition that I have had from my youth. Our marriage is more important than eating German food for dinner. You realize pretty quickly that the relationship won't die if you have to change some of your practices.

But, I really love listening to her. Her life growing up was so different—I really enjoy hearing her talk of life in China as a child. She talks about her culture, her upbringing, and her family. I particularly enjoy her stories of her associations with dissidents in her college years and her involvement in the history and evolution of China. It is fascinating.

Juergen is open to influence. He is fascinated by the cultural differences and revels in how different his wife's perspective and background are. As he has backed off and adopted his wife's practices, he has found that she is doing the same for him. If one of them bends in her or his views, the other will not be so forceful. If one of them compromises one time, the other will compromise the next. *They have discovered that there is nothing so persuasive as being persuaded, and nothing so influential as being influenced.* They both work at meeting in the middle, enjoying their differences and appreciating each other's uniqueness. In a real sense, being open to influence is a power in that it influences others around you to be open to your influence.

Being influenced is the first step to being persuaded that we may not be wearing the right clothes—or any clothes, for that matter. Being open to influence is fundamental to realizing the second side of this same coin: the power of apology.

I will always remember a time when I got really angry at my son. I don't remember what he had done. All I remember is feeling a swelling anger in my gut that erupted into an adult temper tantrum, with angry words that I later wished I could recall. He was only 7 or 8 at the time. I knew instantly that I was wrong in my response. I knew it even as the words came out of my mouth. But they had escaped, and I could not take them back. What was done was done. Or was it? It took me only a moment to know what I should do. I sucked in my egotistical gut and said, 'I am sorry.' That did not seem right yet. I bent down to his level, dropping one knee to the ground, and gently pulled him toward me, sitting him on the thigh of my other leg. We were looking eye to eye. I told him with all the feelings of my heart that I was sorry for getting angry. I told him it was not right for me to get mad, that what he had done was not such a big deal. I could see the tears welling up in his eyes and he grasped me around the neck. I loved that hug. I have to admit that tears were streaming down my cheeks.

I somehow felt immensely different. One moment earlier, I had felt an almost uncontrollable rage that seemed to possess my mind and heart. It literally had a gripping control of what I was thinking and doing. I was amazed at how out of control I really felt at the moment I gave in to my angry impulse.

Now, not even 2 minutes later, how could I feel so elated? A real power came over me—a feeling of strength and of virtue and of doing something right. I don't remember ever having my feelings turn around 180 degrees in such a short time. I came to understand the power of a sincere apology on my feelings and attitude. Years later, as my children grew into teens, I also came to realize that an apology softened and mollified even the toughest teenager. The feeling and power of an apology was not just felt in my heart, but could also be truly felt in the heart of the person with whom I was seeking reconciliation.

In the 1970s, a popular movie called *Love Story* institutionalized one phrase. Ali McGraw played a woman who, in the last stages of her terminal cancer, told her lover and partner, "Love means never having to say you're sorry." The phrase caught on, we hope, in part because of the ridiculousness of the concept. In our view and experience, love means recognizing when you have wronged someone, even if unintentionally. Love means always having to say you're sorry, always being open to learning how to improve, always recognizing that we make mistakes and that we have the wonderful opportunity to forgive and be forgiven. As a wise person once said, "He who is offended when offense was intended is a fool, and he who is offended when offense was not intended is a greater fool."

Happy Days was an extremely popular TV show set in the fifties and starring Ron Howard, with Henry Winkler as "the Fonz." Fonzie, the egotistical but big-hearted biker, was our caricature of the emperor with his new clothes and the delusion of infallibility. During the entire run of the show, Fonzie had a difficult time saying he was sorry. Anytime he tried to say he was sorry, he would stutter almost uncontrollably: "I-I-I-I m-m-m-m-m uh-uh-uh. . . ." He couldn't get the words out. He was right almost all the time, and he had an almost impossible time recognizing when he was wrong—he had a mental and physical block against it. We are all a stuttering Fonzie at times.

As we will discuss later, an apology can open the door and jump-start some sincere fence-mending, *even when we are not at fault.* Nothing accelerates personal change and getting on track toward your own personal legacy than a sincere and heartfelt apology for having hurt someone else, intentionally or not.

There are three main reasons why a sincere apology can be so powerful:

1. *An apology is powerful because it places an emphasis on the long-term value of the relationship, not the value of the immediate action that caused offense.*

A woman described her interaction with her daughter and the ensuing argument, which ended with her daughter's slapping her across the face. The mother was furious at her daughter's behavior—at her belligerence and her disrespect. She had actually slapped her mother. When the mother sought advice on how to deal with the situation, a trusted friend told her to apologize. "What!? Apologize?? I did nothing wrong!!" The mother's initial reaction to the advice was that an apology was not warranted; she had not been in the wrong—in fact, she had been wronged by being slapped by her daughter. She thought how con-

73

trary the advice must be to the common view of how to deal with children's misbehavior. But her friend told her, "You need to apologize for your part in creating a problem in the relationship. The long-term relationship is what is important, not the slap."

The mother mustered her courage, swallowed her pride, and apologized to her daughter for her role in creating the argument. She expressed her love for her daughter and her desire to have a loving relationship with her. She said nothing about what her daughter had done or her belief that her daughter had been totally out of line in her actions. The apology opened the door to resolving the original problem and helped repair the relationship.

We are not suggesting that parents or spouses ignore abusive or hurtful behavior toward them. We are suggesting that we need to be more open to how our role in a situation has created a problem with the relationship. We need to place a high value on the long-term relationship and to be willing to apologize for our role in hurting or bringing disharmony to the relationship.

2. *An apology can elevate our spouse and our children to the role of being our personal coach or consultant.*

An apology can open the door for the individual to be our coach and help us to improve our behavior. Some of the best advice and counsel comes from those who are most familiar with our weaknesses and foibles. They are the ones who love us the most and would love to have an even closer relationship with us. They are the ones who see how we can improve more clearly than we may. They know what bothers them and what creates friction in the relationship. We can't find a person who is in a better position to provide us with helpful coaching and consultation than someone who loves us, knows us, and wants to see us improve.

An apology can say, in effect, "I know I mess things up sometimes, but I would really appreciate your help in being a better person." An apology opens up the hearts of individuals to accept and receive help from each other. It also opens the heart to working collaboratively to improve the relationship.

3. *An apology can restore long-term friendships in the home, which can prevent bigger problems from developing.*

When we have humbly approached a spouse or a child to apologize, there is an almost magical moment that occurs after the awkward humble moment of apologizing. Our openness and willingness to apologize brings feelings of stronger friendship to the family. Ask your spouse or your child how he or she felt the last time you apologized and you will catch a glimpse of the magical power of sincere apology. Perry's daughter Breanne gave the following description, captured in the words of a 14-year-old:

> I can recall many different situations when my father has apologized to me. Some people might see this as a father lowering himself and his stature to apologize to his teenage daughter. But that is not the case. I do not remember the exact situation or what each of us did to cause tension in the home. He was probably not even wrong, but justified in his cause to keep me safe and happy. But what I do remember is what he said to me. He apologized for acting the way he did. Not only did he teach me that day how important the simple phrase, "I'm sorry" really was, but he bettered our relationship with each other. My dad was not lowering himself to apologize to me, but raising himself up in character.
>
> An apology can solve problems between me and my father and erase the memory of our differences, and it can boost my opinion of my father. An apology helps to enhance our friendship and relationship.

My daughter and I have had our differences of opinion. She doesn't like my being "overprotective," and I don't like some of her stubborn displays of independence. But we love each other, apologize when needed, and we try to keep our relationship on our mind all the time, despite our differences.

EXERCISE: *How Lost Are You in Behavioral Fog?*

At times, all of us are lost in behavioral fog. We think and act in ways that take a short-term perspective on our relationships. We forget that our relationships with our family and other close relationships are meant to last a lifetime. A father doesn't cease to be a father when his child leaves home. A mother doesn't cease to be a mother when her child gets married. A brother doesn't cease to be a sibling to his sister even though they have offended each other. As one woman from the U.K. said to us, "The nice thing is that it doesn't matter how old they are, they still involve me in their problems. It is a compliment that they come to me. But their problems never stop hurting me more than they hurt them. Once a mother, always a mother, and they want a piece of me. I kind of like that."

So, how lost do you get in behavioral fog? Consider the following questions.

Instant Gratification Questions

- When I see something I like, do I tend to buy it, even if it is a little beyond my means?
- Do I tend to expect my spouse to immediately follow my advice?
- Do I tend to be impatient when my children are not immediately obedient to my wishes?
- Do I grow impatient when I cannot overcome some of my character weaknesses quickly?
- Do I become frustrated when my investments don't quickly yield the return I think they should?

The Law of Diminishing Returns Questions

- As I become older, do I seem to be more successful and invest more time at work than with my family?
- Do I feel like giving up on one or more of the members of my family because they are not accomplishing what I think they should accomplish?

- Do I feel exhausted when I have to deal with a perplexing and challenging personal issue in my family?
- Do I consistently feel friction and contention with at least one member of my immediate or extended family?
- Do I feel like giving up on a relationship with at least one immediate or extended family member because I am doubtful that the relationship can be improved?

The Delusion of Infallibility: The Emperor's New Clothes

- Do I feel that I give great advice and have a history of accurate judgments?
- Do I generally create the rules in our home, with little or no input from other family members?
- Do I become irritated when someone criticizes me?
- Is it difficult for me to ask forgiveness of family members?
- Is it difficult for me to recognize and willingly admit when I have done something wrong?

The Three Pillars of Behavior

Our work with thousands of people over the years has helped to shape a model of effective behavior. What are the behaviors we need to have in order to build and maintain strong personal relationships? Which behaviors are most critical, which behaviors will make the most difference, and how effective are most people in implementing these behaviors? These are some of the questions that we have begun to answer as we have built and shaped the Family 360 process.

The Family 360 survey and assessment process is based on three clusters of behaviors. These behaviors form the three pillars of effective and strong personal relationships. As with a three-legged stool, the absence of any one pillar can result in the entire structure collapsing.

Consequently, individuals need to have some degree of competency in each of the three pillars in order to have a good relationship. Each one provides for the stability of the relationship. Let's explore each of these pillars in more detail. They form the basis for the questions we will be asking in the Family 360 survey in Chapters 8 through 10.

Core Behaviors

Core behaviors are those behaviors that are fundamental to a strong personal relationship: communication, listening, effective problem solving, support, and respect. A successful dentist described his regrets at not focusing on core behaviors in his family:

> Throughout my school and professional career, I have been recognized for my accomplishments. I received a perfect score on my SAT test. (Ironically, when I showed my father my test score, he asked if I could have done better—he was like that.) I graduated with straight A's in my undergraduate degree and went on to receive two master's degrees and one Ph.D., all with honors. I finally received a Doctor of Dentistry. My practice has been widely recognized, and I have been asked to be a member of a prestigious peer review board, a board that reviews malpractice cases against dentists.
>
> I did an analysis of the time I spend on different activities during my normal week. I spend on average 71 hours on the job, 10 hours commuting, and many hours at home studying to stay on top of the latest advances in dentistry. The remaining time is spent recuperating from my work effort. I spend all my prime time consumed in making money. I drive an old car and don't live extravagantly, but I find that all my time is required in order to save money for my eight children and their education. Next year, five of them will be in college at the same time, one at Cornell.
>
> The other day I received my Father's Day cards. And then it really hit me. My children expressed their love for me, and then they all independently told me how much they admired my hard work, the hours I spent at the office, my work ethic. Not one of them mentioned appreciation for time I spent with them. That's because I really left that up to

my wife. I have so many regrets. If I were to do it all over again, I would spend time and just talk, listen, and ask a lot of questions. I would just try to get to know my children better.

Core behaviors are those characteristics or behaviors that are basic and fundamental in most relationships. Without these basic elements, relationships are weak or strained and will not flourish and grow. It is upon these core behaviors that lasting and strong relationships are built. The core behaviors measured in the Family 360 survey are:

- *Communicating and listening.* Listening, taking the time to communicate, understanding concerns and personal feelings, asking questions, getting to know your spouse and your children
- *Problem solving.* Finding fair solutions to disagreements, without getting angry
- *Support.* Providing the basic necessities of life and a secure home environment
- *Equal partnership and respect.* Valuing and respecting each person's role

Relationship Behaviors

Relationship behaviors are those behaviors that help the relationship flourish and grow: demonstrating love, spending quantity and quality time, keeping commitments, and having fun. A CEO of a *Fortune* 200 corporation described a turning point for him with his relationship behaviors:

Quality does not make up for quantity—you need more time, not less. I learned that with my daughter several years ago. One weekend we went to the beach in Cape May. My daughter was 3 or 4 at the time. Even though I was down there on vacation, I was on the phone; I was meeting people for business over tennis. I was busy all the time. My daughter just treated me really cold; she didn't treat me like her father. It was really weird.

I was out with her one day, and she got sick. She threw up all over herself. I took care of her. I took her inside and gave her a bath. I spent about 2 hours with her, talking with her and helping her feel comfortable again. She didn't feel well, she was embarrassed, and we were alone; her mother wasn't there. But after that time together, her feeling toward me totally changed. She wanted to be with me. We talked and had fun together.

We had experienced that one little moment together. The memory and the feeling stuck in my mind, and the next year I told all my business friends, "I'm not going to dinner; I'm not playing tennis; I'm just going to play with the kids on vacation." Then you take them to the pool and instead of looking at your watch for when you need to get back to a meeting, you jump into the pool with them and have a good time. The fact is, you have a really good time.

A long time ago, I decided that out of work, family, and golf, I could pick two things. I picked family and work. I wanted to improve my relationship with my family, which takes time. Your priorities have to be right—you have to be prepared to decide to spend time where you need to spend time. The most difficult part of the balance is when you change jobs; when you have to be immersed in a new job, there is never enough time. Early in my career I was one of the few people sent to California to establish our business when it was fairly new. I had to consciously say, "I'm not spending enough time with my family, including my two daughters, and I need to do something about it."

As our CEO experienced, relationship behaviors are those actions and attitudes that build upon and strengthen the core behaviors. They foster the development of richness, depth, and love in a relationship. They require a greater investment of time and energy, yet they yield a much greater return on personal investment. Relationship behaviors require a greater commitment in both outward expressions and less visible attitudes. The key relationship behaviors measured in the Family 360 survey are:

- *Demonstrating love.* Showing love through words and actions
- *Integrity.* Keeping commitments and respecting others
- *Dedicating time.* Finding the time to give to prime relationships
- *Fun and humor.* Displaying an appropriate sense of humor

Growth Behaviors

Anna was the daughter of a Dutch dairy farmer who had migrated from Europe years earlier to establish a small but thriving dairy farm. She described the difficult and long hours that were a way of life for dairy farmers. "Dairy cows have to be milked twice a day, every day. As a result, we got up at 6 A.M. and worked through to 8 or 9 at night. And that was every day except Sunday, when we awoke at 4 A.M., worked through 10 in the morning and then had a break, and went back to milk the second time at 4 P.M. and worked until 9 that night."

If the cows were milked on schedule, 200 cows could produce 11,000 gallons of milk each day. If a cow was missed for some reason, the milk would thicken and spoil, and the cow would require 3 or 4 days to become productive again. Needless to say, the family worked hard. When school was in session, Anna worked as much as possible during the time she was not spending at school or doing homework. Her mother and father picked up the slack. Vacation consisted of 1 week per year with the family while a cousin or relative milked the cows in their place. We asked about their relationship as a family. "We have gotten very close as a family since we came over 5 years ago and started the dairy farm." What was the reason for their being so close? "We worked together—that is how we stayed close. We had to make the farm work. In addition, because we worked together, we also had all our meals together—breakfast, lunch, and dinner. We went out occasionally for birthday parties and the Fourth of July, but mainly our closeness comes from working together." Anna also credits her father and mother for being very supportive of their children's decisions, whether it was the oldest daughter's decision to stay in Holland or the youngest daughter's decision to go to college and leave the family farm. Her father was an effective counselor, and he helped his children understand their strengths and develop their talents.

As the example of Anna's father illustrates, growth behaviors are the "enhancing" actions driven by our deep personal beliefs and values. They are the additional efforts we make in order to teach, build, and encourage the development of personal character, ethics, a sense of worth, and values.

They are the behaviors that not only deepen the strength of the individual and the family, but also put into perspective the importance of the family unit in society (even if the family unit consists of only two people).

- *Sense of purpose.* Showing the importance of the family unit in helping and serving each other, building traditions, instilling values, and contributing to society
- *Complimenting, building, and encouraging.* Motivating family members to develop their talents and to achieve a higher level

Chapters 8 through 10 will describe the Family 360 survey process that builds on the three pillars of behavior and gives powerful feedback on ways that will improve our personal and family relationships.

Summary of the Thinking and Behavioral Success Factors

In Chapters 3 and 4 we have outlined some of the common elements and "ailments" that we have found in counseling many busy people. The ailments are in both our way of thinking and our way of behaving. Each influences the other: The way we think influences the way we behave, and the way we behave influences the way we think. The remedy lies in changing our thinking and behaving through several entry points, as the diagram on page 83 illustrates.

Further, human beings are wonderful creatures who can be programmed and reprogrammed. The adage "you can't teach an old dog new tricks" was obviously meant for dogs, not for people. We firmly believe that humans are the most resilient and reprogrammable species on the planet. We can think and reason and deliberately set and strive for goals. We can feel things deeply and can think about and analyze how we are feeling. We can bounce back from catastrophe and heartache and despair. We have seen people who have taught themselves to think in different ways and to behave in different ways. As the following table shows, we can move from having an

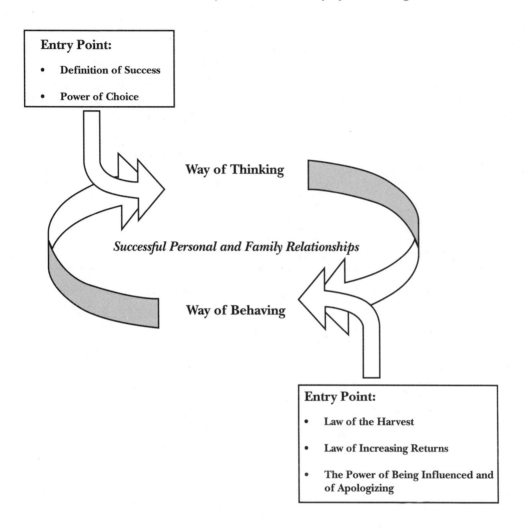

Entry Point:

- **Definition of Success**

- **Power of Choice**

Way of Thinking

Successful Personal and Family Relationships

Way of Behaving

Entry Point:

- Law of the Harvest

- Law of Increasing Returns

- The Power of Being Influenced and of Apologizing

imbalanced definition of success to a position of creating, thinking, and acting on a balanced definition of success. We can move from the position of feeling that things are outside our control to a position of having influence over them through our choice. And we can move from a position of feeling falsely infallible to a position of being able to readily apologize and to be influenced by others.

Clearing the Thinking Fog		
		Critical Success Factors
Imbalanced definition of success: the tendency to define success in terms of work achievement	⇨	**Rebalanced definition of success:** the process of balancing work achievement with achievements in personal relationships
Situation outside of our control: the tendency to think that factors outside of our control determine our situation	⇨	**Reprogrammed power of choice:** the process of realizing the amount of control we have over work and personal inhibitors—and acting on that realization

Clearing the Behavioral Fog		
Instant gratification: the tendency to want instant results	⇨	**The law of the harvest:** the habit of nurturing and developing relationships
The law of diminishing returns: the tendency to stop trying after we reach a peak investment of time and energy	⇨	**The law of increasing returns:** the habit of continual, long-term investment of effort to build a relationship
The delusion of infallibility—the emperor's new clothes: the tendency to act as if we are infallible, placing excessive trust in our capabilities and not recognizing our need to seek forgiveness	⇨	**The power of being influenced:** the habit of being open to new ideas and perspectives **The power of apologizing:** the habit of asking forgiveness when we do something wrong

Finally, we have identified three clusters of behaviors that form the basis for effective and strong personal relationships. Individuals need a minimum competency in each behavior pillar in order to have a stable relationship. The Family 360 instrument in Chapters 8 through 10 will help provide you with feedback on how well you are doing in each of the pillars.

CHAPTER 5

Getting Started: Creating and Living Your Legacy Now

"What we call the beginning is often the end. And to make an end is to make a beginning. The end is where we start from."

—T. S. Eliot

"THAT WAS ONE of the most difficult, trying times of my life," the executive (we will call him John) told us as he described the personal and mental turmoil he had recently experienced. John had literally experienced more major life changes in 4 months than most people experience in 20 years. He had just made a job change that required a transition from working with one company in one state to joining another company in another state. This was a particularly difficult move for his family. Not only did it require the family to move in the cold of winter in the middle of the school year, but, more significantly, it came at a time when they had just lost a baby daughter.

On John's first day on his new job, he went to take the company physical exam. After a series of tests and x-rays, the doctor came into the room and said, "We have reviewed your chest x-rays, and you have a spot on one of your lungs." The doctor went on to explain that he had either pneumonia or lung cancer. John was devastated. He knew that he was run down after the funeral of his daughter, but he didn't feel ill. Needless to say, he was fearful of the worst scenario. The possibility of cancer preyed on his mind in a very significant way.

John described how he went on to closely examine all aspects of his life: his work, his family relationships, his standing with his God. A thousand questions raced across his mind: "If I had only 3 months or even 3 years to live, would I be doing what I am doing at work? Would I be satisfied with what I have done on the home front? Would I be pleased with what others, especially the members of my family, would say about the relationship I had with them? How would I be remembered by those I cared for most? What would they say about me as an individual?" The executive thought deeply about his own personal "legacy"—what he wanted to contribute to his family, how he wanted to be remembered, and what he could pass on to future generations.

Over a period of 4 months, John anguished over the answers to these questions as the doctors debated their diagnosis. During that time, he spent a lot of time defining the legacy that he wanted, particularly for his family. He spent a lot of time in introspection, recommitment, and renewal, hoping that if he made it through this challenge, he would make some big changes in his life. He took the time to clearly identify what was really important in his life and translated those thoughts and aspirations into actual behaviors. He carefully examined where his current behavior was falling short. For the first time he truly had a clear picture of what he really wanted and what he needed to do in order to improve (to close the gap between his ideal and his current actions).

John told us that his greatest insight during that 4 months was that, although he had progressed quickly in his corporate career and was making more than sufficient money, he was still unhappy. He was unhappy because he had neglected to invest in the one thing that really brought him true happiness—his relationship with his family. He spoke with his spouse about his resolve and made some firm commitments to make significant changes in his work habits, and also, more importantly, in his relationships with his family. The good news was that the doctors eventually let him know that he only had pneumonia. Unfortunately, it took the entire 4 months to get that confirmation. In hindsight, as difficult as it had been to be in limbo for 4 months, he had had a life-changing experience as he redefined what he wanted to leave his family as his legacy: what he wanted to become as a person and as a husband and father, and what behavior he needed to adopt to achieve that legacy. *And, more important, John began living his legacy.*

John's experience provides a good overview of the process of establishing a legacy:

1. He had a deep inner conversation about his highest priorities.
2. He wrote his commitments down and shared them with his wife and family.
3. Finally, he started acting on his commitments and trying to live his legacy.

What We Have Learned about "Legacy" from Working with Leaders

Much of our expertise in coaching individuals on personal and family relationships has come out of our experience in coaching leaders in many capacities, many of whom experience painful personal relationships. Over the years we have coached people in work, government, and community settings and raised the question of their own "leadership legacy" in their work setting. We ask them to visualize a time when they are at the end of their careers and to look back over time and ask:

- What did I accomplish as a leader?
- What were my most significant contributions as a leader?
- What will those who knew me best remember about me as time goes on?

These reflections on leadership legacy can easily be applied in a personal way. Ben was in North Carolina conducting a leadership development program at the well-known Pinehurst golf resort. After an early morning jog, he had these reflections:

At the Pinehurst golf resort in North Carolina, there are a number of statues and monuments that have been erected over the years honoring some of the great professional golfers and war heroes of the past.

87

One statue, erected on the 18th hole of the Number Two golf course, was particularly poignant to me. It is a statue of Payne Stewart that captures the personality and vitality for life that he had throughout his career, and particularly after his final putt that won him the 1999 U.S. Open. Tragically, he died 4 months later in an airplane accident, leaving behind a wife and children. As I saw this statue one morning while jogging, I couldn't help but think what would happen if I suddenly died, too. What monuments would be erected in the hearts and minds of my wife and children? Would they remember me for always working, being away from home, and being impatient or preoccupied when I was home? Or would they remember me for having fun, being loving and caring, and spending time with them? Would they remember me for the legacy I would like to leave them, or would their memory be more like the "tomb of the unknown father"?

Eventually, everyone will hang up his or her career boots and leave the organization in which he or she invested a lot of time. We believe it is helpful to ask people to think about that time *today* and to think about how they would want to leave it behind, what they would want to be known for, and what contributions they would like to have remembered.

As we coach people on leadership in a company, it is clear that very few have spent much time thinking about their personal leadership legacy in any real depth. Unfortunately, those who are at the twilight of their careers take this question much more seriously than most others. The only difficulty with waiting until the tail end of our career is that we end up fulfilling our legacy by chance. *Legacy is all about today.* It is all about clarifying in our minds what we must do today to successfully fulfill the aspirations we have for the future. Too often we live for the here and now. Many of us are too focused on what we can get out of the current situation, rather than thinking about how we can really add long-lasting value, how we can repay what others have done for us, and how we can share the lessons of our leadership experience with those who are coming behind us.

In essence, there is a real gap in thinking about our legacy. We all feel that it is important, but we do not take enough time to fully develop our legacy early in our career. As a result, when we are not clear about what we feel is important to have at the end of our career, we miss big opportunities along the way to act on what we believe to be critically important.

There is also another type of gap when it comes to legacy. This gap occurs when we do not behave according to what we want our legacy to be. We have conducted many coaching sessions in which we have given an individual feedback about the effectiveness of her or his leadership practices in her or his current job. Many of these people realize for the first time that they will not achieve their desired legacy if they continue to behave the way they are behaving today. The next step in our conversation centers on the identification of behaviors that make a difference—the kinds of behaviors that will move one closer to achieving a leadership legacy.

Many of our conversations start with these individuals relating to us contributions, attributes, or characteristics that they would like to be known for by others. We then push them to describe how these aspirations can be translated into behaviors. If we cannot describe what we want to become or achieve in behavioral terms, it will be very difficult for us to know if we are making progress or if we will ever reach our desired state. It will be difficult for us to take action or improve on anything if we cannot first put it in terms that can be acted on. For example, it is one thing to say, "I want to be a great leader," and quite another to say, "I want to be able to effectively give my direct reports candid, balanced feedback about their performance."

The Reciprocal Nature of Work and Family

Our work to improve leadership in corporations through our candid leadership feedback goes hand in hand with our Family 360 process to provide candid feedback from the home. Our Family 360 coaching is, in essence, personal and family relationship leadership. In our Family 360 coaching, we take individuals through the same line of leadership thinking for their personal and family relationships. We ask leaders to think about and clarify the legacy they want to live in their families, and we also ask them to clarify the legacy they would like to leave with their families. We have found that a leadership legacy and a personal and family legacy go hand in hand with each other.

One reason for this close relationship between work and personal life is that much of what happens at work flows over into the family setting. Conversely, what happens or does not happen on the home front flows back to the work setting. We feel that taking a holistic approach in our coaching efforts makes a big difference in helping people to be happy and well-balanced people and happy and well-balanced workers.

Note how some prominent businesspeople express this reciprocal influence of work and family:

- **Fortune *50 executive*.** "It's foolish to believe that people who are unfulfilled in their personal life will be able to turn it off like a toggle switch when they walk through the doors of the company. So, to the degree that you can add fulfillment to their life, you're helping them add value to their employer."
- *Asia Pacific business director.* "There is a real commitment to the work ethic in Asia. That makes it harder to have a mental balance. I work to ensure that there is a mental balance. I am convinced that unless the family is happy, the employee will not be a 'happy camper.' It will be detrimental to the job."
- *Japanese businessperson.* "I have my family and my own personal life. If there is imbalance, the most important thing in my life is destroyed. I worry about that. That situation would influence my work. I would like to live a happy family life. If I live a happy family life, I can do a good job."
- *U.S. businessperson.* "When there are problems at work, there is a spillover to the home, and when there are problems with the home, there is a spillover to the work. Both work and family should be able to enrich each other—a person should be enriched by both experiences."

Creating Your Family Legacy and Living It Now

The same approach that is used to develop a leadership legacy for our work responsibilities can also be used to develop and live a personal and family legacy, with one major difference: A family legacy is far more important than a work legacy. One CEO of a major corporation described the need to have a personal legacy and start living it now: "On your deathbed, are you going to say, 'Thank God I worked that extra weekend in September or November of 1994'? You won't. You will say, if you have kids, 'That trip or that vacation or that road trip, that was memorable!' And on your deathbed you may say that that was one of the very best times in your life. Which is what I would say about a lot of trips I've gone on with my kids."

Patti Davis, the daughter of former president Ronald Reagan, eloquently described how her father's family legacy and example of love means more to her now than any political legacy he may have left:

> We think differently about days that have been set aside to honor our parents—Mother's Day, Father's Day—which once were just reasons to go buy cards or gifts, but later take on deeper meaning. We pause on those days, overwhelmed by a surprising surge of reverence for the task our parents took on: bringing us into the world and trying their best to get it right.
>
> There are people who would say that my father's footprints are larger and deeper than those of other parents because his political legacy gives them weight, creating indelible marks in the halls of history. But those aren't the footprints I see when I look back down the years. I see the soft scuff of dirt rising up from his brown walking shoes as he took his daughter to the top of the hill to fly a kite. . . . I see his footprints pressed into the wet sand of the beach as he walked toward the sea. . . . His stride was as smooth and certain as it was when he walked into the White House, and onto the stage of history. I see a small girl on that beach as well, pressing her feet into the shapes that her father's feet have left to see how much bigger his footprints are.
>
> I have gotten lost in those footprints during my life; I have fought hard and bloody battles to pull myself away [from the family]. These are the tracks I have left on the earth. But now I look for my father's tracks on every beach, every trail. Because they mark the way home. ("I'm Ready to Follow My Father's Lead," *Newsweek*, July 16, 2003)

Patti Davis describes reality for the majority of us: In the end, our relationship with our family is more dependent on the family legacy we have forged than on the public accolades we have received.

Personal and Family Legacy: A Vision of Whom We Want to Become

We find that many of the people whom we work with have not taken a lot of time to meaningfully think through the legacy that they want to leave in the hearts and minds of their family by the end of their life. They know that it is important, but they have been so caught up in the challenges of the day that they arrive at the end of their life having missed the big opportunities to identify and fulfill their legacy to their families.

Of those who have thought through their personal and family legacy, many have found that it is hard to express their desired contributions in behavioral terms—behaviors that they can observe and monitor to determine whether they are making a difference for their family. Without a legacy that is grounded in actual behavior, we will find it difficult to compare our legacy against the behaviors we currently demonstrate.

Examples of Personal and Family Legacy

Here is a sampling of how busy people, just like you, have started to describe and capture in writing some of the ways they want to live their legacy.

Core Behaviors: Communicating, Listening, Problem Solving, Supporting, and Respecting

- "I want to be sought out for my advice and sensitive listening long after the children have left the family."
- "I want to be known as someone who created a feeling of love and acceptance in our home, where the children can come and feel safe, wanted, and needed."

- "I would like to be remembered as someone who treated my family with respect and dignity and who did not 'dis' people, as my kids would say."
- "I want them to say that I gave them good advice. After my children leave the home, we won't see them every weekend because life will be more hectic than today. I wouldn't want to impose on their time, but I would like to have a good relationship with them even after they are grown."
- "I want to be remembered as someone who truly listened."
- "I would like to be known as someone who was continually trustworthy, whom they could talk to, and who would keep a confidence. Like a Duracell battery, I want to be known for my constancy—that I keep going and going."
- "My goal is to fully appreciate my wife and her style, and to treat her the way she would want to be treated."
- "I want to look back and to say with my wife, 'We have had lots of good times together. We derived a lot of joy out of the things we did together. We had a good life, and we accomplished what we wanted.'"

Relationship Behaviors of Demonstrating Love and Dedicating Time

- "I want to be known as a warm, personal mom who was there when my children needed me. I want to be the same role model that my mother was and is to me."
- "I want my husband to remember us as best friends. I want him to remember me not only as his wife and lover, but as his best friend."
- "I would not worry about the number of times they think I said 'I love you,' but could they feel my love, did they know it, did I demonstrate love?"
- "I want to be remembered as always making time for the family, even when I was busy."
- "I want my legacy to be one of being loving, caring, and supporting, and having a sense of humor."
- "I want them to remember that I was always there for them. That includes my husband—that I was always there for him and supportive of what he wanted to do."

- "I want them to know that when I am around, I can help. The true acid test will be whether my children will feel that they can come to me for anything, especially in their adolescence."
- "I want to be known as an anchor of joy, someone they enjoy spending time with, can have good open dialogue with, and can have fun times with."

Growth Behaviors of Creating a Sense of Purpose and Encouraging Contribution

- "I want to contribute to my family and children being happy and productive."
- "I want my family to think that I have helped them grow and become better people—that I helped them learn and develop as people."
- "Life is an adventure. I want to be remembered as someone who encourages others to live life as an adventure."
- "I want to be remembered as encouraging continual learning. There's always something to learn."
- "For my kids, I want them to remember me as someone who has helped prepare them for life, as someone who helped them in their growing-up years to take on all the challenges of life."
- "I would want my children to say, 'Here was a guy who assisted me in getting somewhere that I wanted to go in my life, who was a source of knowledge and inspiration, and who helped me be successful in life.' I would not want to get to a spot in 10 years and have them say, 'My life is completely screwed up, and you are the cause of it.' I would hope they see the opposite."
- "I would want them to say that I am an example, a beacon of how to live a good life. They could use me as the role model for that person."
- "I want my family to say, 'The values my mother taught and lived by are the values I now want to teach my children.'"
- "I want to live life with no regrets about how I raised my family and developed my children."

- "I like to build capability in my kids. It is a real highlight when they say once a month or so, 'I got an A.' I like being involved in making them a success, especially with their schoolwork."
- "I want to be known as someone who is building family memories, even long after the children are gone from the home."
- "I want to have the reputation of bringing the family together, of bridging generations and reconciling differences."
- "I want to be known for creating memorable experiences that live in the minds and hearts of my family."
- "I want to be remembered for teaching my children to love God, themselves, and their neighbor, and to love to learn and to be socially responsible."

Our challenge to all who are reading this book is not to wait for the threat of death, old age, or a significant emotional event to think through and act on one's personal legacy to his or her family. Now is the time to create and act on your legacy. It is as simple as doing some serious inner reflection about how you want to be known, translating your reflections into specific behaviors, and gathering feedback on your legacy, goals, and behaviors from those who matter most in your life. Finally, living your legacy now means starting to live as if your legacy were already a fact.

The following exercises describe the easiest and most effective ways to develop your own personal legacy.

EXERCISE 5A: *Personal and Family Legacy—Creating Your Legacy*

We will run through a series of three exercises and ask that you complete your answers on the form found at the end of this chapter. Your answers should be written under the column corresponding to the exercise below (e.g., Exercise 5A, 5B, or 5C).

Creating a family legacy begins with asking yourself a few soul-searching questions.

- Take a few moments to think about the following four questions and jot down your ideas in the space provided.

- Then, when you have jotted down your thoughts on each of the questions, write a few summarizing statements that answer each question in the left-hand column of the form labeled Exercise 5A.

  1. What do you want to be remembered for by your spouse and by your children?

  2. How would you want your spouse and your children to describe the relationship they had with you at the end of your life?

  3. What behavior would they say best demonstrated your love for them?

4. How would you want them to describe your strengths or the qualities or attributes that they most respected?

Once you have completed your first pass at answering these questions, you may want to think about them, and perhaps even sleep on them for a day. You may find that your thinking begins to become clearer and your priorities become more easily articulated.

EXERCISE 5B: *Personal and Family Legacy: Linking Your Legacy to Your Actual Behavior*

The next level of specificity will require you to take each of the contributions, attributes, and/or characteristics that you identified and ask yourself how it is or will be manifested in terms of behavior. How will you actually behave? Return to the form and complete the center column, labeled Exercise 5B, by asking yourself the question, "How can I achieve my legacy—what do I actually have to do?" Use the questions listed below to help you think through the behaviors that are most important to your own personal and family legacy.

1. *Core behaviors.* How can I create my legacy by achieving results in the basics of family life? For example:

   - How can I communicate more effectively?
   - How can I listen more sincerely and pay attention to personal feelings?
   - How can I help resolve problems fairly and without getting angry?
   - How can I show respect for my spouse and my children?
   - How can I contribute more fairly to the home tasks?

2. *Relationship behaviors.* How can I develop deep and meaningful relationships? For example:

- How can I be more effective at demonstrating my love?
- How can I program myself to always use a kind voice?
- How can I be a true friend to my spouse and to my children?
- What can I do to schedule and participate in more important events for my children and my spouse?
- How can I develop the habit of apologizing when I am wrong or have hurt someone's feelings?
- How can I be better at keeping promises to spend more time with the family?
- In what ways can I spend special one-on-one time with my spouse?
- In what ways can I spend special one-on-one time with my children?
- How can I create more fun and memorable activities with the family?

3. *Growth behaviors.* How can I develop capability within my family—create a sense of purpose, develop character, and instill values? For example:

- What can I do to help my family feel more united?
- How can I show that my personal relationships are more important than my work?
- How can I encourage the family to love and serve others?
- What can I do to encourage our family to work together?
- What traditions should we create in our family?
- How can I be more effective at teaching and role modeling good values?

It is important that you start by making a long list of behavioral descriptors, but then cut the list back. Eventually, you should lock onto a few key behaviors that you feel are the real differentiators that best describe how you want to be remembered.

Write your behavioral descriptors in the column for Exercise 5B.

EXERCISE 5C: *Personal and Family Legacy: Getting Input on Your Legacy*

Spend some time thinking through what it really means to become the person you have described in the first two columns. Then it is time to let your family "audit" your list of behaviors in Exercise 5C.

The last step in developing a personal and family legacy is sharing it with others to get some feedback about what you have identified. We recommend that you share this with your spouse first to get her or his reactions to what you have identified. Your spouse will be very helpful not only in identifying blind spots, but also helping you understand where you do things very well. We also recommend that you share it with your children. They can be very helpful in identifying what they would like you to do differently. Return to the form and complete the right-hand column to include the input from your spouse and your children.

Keep in mind that while it is helpful to share your thoughts with others, this legacy is yours. It should come from the heart and the gut—*your* gut and your heart.

Now that you have the beginnings of your own legacy, you have a target to shoot for—a goal that can help shape your thinking and behaving. Your legacy should be written down and available for regular review. You may want to place a copy in your wallet or purse, or put it in your personal organizer. We recommend that you review it everyday for at least 1 month and regularly thereafter. Commit it to memory. Review it with your spouse and with your children. Ask them whether you are making progress toward your desired legacy.

Once you have formulated the legacy that you want to leave your family, the next step is to match the statements with those behaviors that you currently practice. This will help you to understand whether you are on track or whether there is a gap between your current behaviors and your desired legacy. We will show you several ways to get good, accurate, and constructive feedback on how you can improve your behavior. This is the purpose of Family 360—to help you get the accurate input you need from your spouse or significant other, children, mom and dad, siblings, grandparents, and close friends. That's coming up in Chapters 7, 8, 9, and 10. Good luck.

Personal and Family Legacy Worksheet

EXERCISE 5A: *Answers to Legacy Questions*	EXERCISE 5B: *Behavior That Will Get You to Your Legacy*	EXERCISE 5C: *Input from Your Personal Friends and/or Family*
Example: *I want to be known for always listening to and loving my family.*	**Example:** *I will walk 20 minutes in the morning with my spouse and spend 30 minutes after work just sitting with the children and talking.*	**Example:** —*Daddy needs to play with me more.* —*John needs to call me during the day to just talk.*
1.		
2.		
3.		
4.		

CHAPTER 6

Leveraging Your Strengths

"Give me a lever long enough and a fulcrum on which to place it, and I shall move the world."

—Archimedes

JEFF HAD PLAYED basketball throughout his life, including on high school and college teams. It was a sport he loved dearly. It had provided him with a sense of accomplishment and confidence among his peers in his earlier years. Now it provided him with a fun way to continue to stay in shape as he moved into his forties. And it was a way for him to stay connected with his two sons. It was not unusual for him to spend two or three evenings a week after work playing basketball with his two sons on the driveway. He spent the time teaching them basketball skills and techniques and the strategy of playing competitively. And they had a lot of fun together skirmishing. He felt that he was providing his boys an avenue to learn skills, develop self-confidence, and prepare to be on their school teams. Plus, it kept them in a good environment. He felt good about that.

He was not prepared for what his Family 360 assessment brought to light. When he sought feedback from his 12-year-old daughter on how he could be a better father, she tearfully told him, "You never play basketball with me." He had been playing exclusively with his sons and was not even aware that his daughter felt neglected. She wanted to play basketball and have some one-on-one time with him, just as much as his sons did. And she wanted to do the very thing that was his strength. Jeff took her up on her request. He started playing basketball with his daughter and had an equally satisfying experience with her. He had leveraged his strength to develop his relationship with another family member.

Why Should We Focus First on Our Strengths?

We live in a world today that tends to gravitate to the negative, the problem, the controversial. We tend to focus on problem behavior, weaknesses, and deficiencies. For example, if our child brings home a report card with one low grade and five higher grades, we tend to focus on what needs to be done to raise the low grade rather than to recognize and build on the five higher grades. Focusing on areas that need improvement serves a purpose, but it is only half the formula when it comes to continuous improvement. We need to focus on our strengths in order to effectively close the gap between where we are and where we want to be. Consider the following principles:

1. *We are more energized to do more of what we already do well.* We all enjoy being recognized for what we do well. From our early years we tend to be more influenced by positive comments from someone we value and love than by negative comments. We like people to recognize our strengths rather than point out our weaknesses. We like to be around positive people who see the positive in us. We tend to be more motivated to act when others recognize our strengths.

2. *We will experience greater success if we play off our strengths.* We already know how to do these things well. We can more easily apply them to a wider variety of people and settings. For example, if we are good at giving compliments and encouraging our children to develop their talents, perhaps we need to apply that strength to our spouse as well as our children. If we are good at problem solving at work, perhaps we can apply our strength from

work to more effectively and collaboratively solve problems at home. Effective personal relationships depend on capitalizing on our strengths and trying to make their use more common in practice.

3. *A positive approach to leveraging our strengths is a brilliant antidote for criticism.* Spouses and children in particular respond to a positive approach to addressing their weaknesses rather than confrontational or condemning criticism of their behavior. For example, one of the teenage daughters in our coaching had this insightful comment about her mother and how the two of them should work out problems differently:

> I wish you were more open about your own personal experiences, so I can learn more about you and more about the way you decided to shape your life. I feel that at the age I'm at, it helps if I know how you would deal with something or why you made certain decisions in your life so I can make good decisions as well. *That is much better than criticizing me so that I can learn from my behavior. Criticism works only if it's done in a positive way.*

Our personal and family relationships can benefit more from our positive experiences than from our criticism or candid feedback.

4. *A positive approach to leveraging strengths will allow skills learned at work to be transferred to our personal relationships.* Some of us have developed skills in our work setting, such as time management, project planning and management, presentation and oral communication skills, problem solving, and analytical competencies. Often we don't share these skills with the people we love most—our family members. How many of us really make an effort to teach the members of our family some of the most important lessons we have learned over the years? For example, we can use our project management skills to plan family vacations and weekend adventures. We can use our time management skills to find lost slivers of time to spend with our children. We can use our analytical skills to help a teenager work through complex homework problems.

We all have strengths, things we do well that others in our family appreciate. We need to build on these strengths and leverage them in our relationships. But more important, everyone has some wonderful strengths and positive aspects of their lives that are immeasurably appreciated. These are the behaviors, traits, and attributes that, bundled together, will propel you toward your personal and family legacy (see the diagram in Chapter 2).

As we discuss strengths in this chapter, we will provide you with comments from individuals who have gone through Family 360 and their perspective on what they view as the strengths of their father, mother, husband, or wife. As you read these comments, you may feel that they all had perfect relationships, strong marriages, and close friendships with their children. That would be a wrong conclusion to reach. And there is a lesson in this: Every one of us does things that are viewed by others with great appreciation and love. Sometimes we don't know what those things are. Sometimes they are buried by a host of negative complaints and criticisms. But if we could tease them out and help them to emerge into the full light of day, we would see how wonderful these positive things are and how much they are appreciated by others. A key point to learn from this chapter is that everyone has challenges and problems in personal and family relationships. We do, you do, and the people we coach do.

The questions that need to be asked are:

1. What do I do well in my relationships with various members of my family?
2. What can I do to leverage those strengths in other personal relationships or relationships with members of my family?

We have found that everyone gets positive feedback from someone in the family. We have seen people demonstrate some wonderful practices with their children, but not with their spouse. Others have developed some very effective habits with their spouse, but have not carried over these habits to their children. Some have behaved in a certain way with their own mother and father, but have not passed along these behaviors to their own immediate family. For example, some have learned to serve their parents and/or their siblings over the years, but have not learned to serve their children to the same degree. We have counseled individuals who would go and help their parents at the drop of a hat if they had a need, but who can't find the time to sit down with their children and help them with their homework. We have worked with people who are very close with a sibling and would always do things with them, but do not consistently spend time with their spouse. We have had many conversations with busy people who will find the time to engage in quality activities with their children, but have not developed or maintained a strong relationship with their spouse. Everyone does some things well in his or her family and personal relationships. The quest for each of us is to identify those strengths and see what we can do to leverage them with other members of the family.

EXERCISE: *Capitalizing on Your Strengths*

This exercise is one of the most important activities in this book. It is easy to do, and it can uncover a wealth of soul-strengthening information. More important, it can provide a clear road map for reaching your family legacy by building on the memories, events, and behavior that have already helped forge some of your memories.

You can do this exercise as a couple or with as many immediate and extended family members as you would like. The purpose of the exercise is to understand how you have contributed to some good memories in the past in order to know how to create future good memories. If you understand the memories, events, and behavior that your family members appreciate the most, you will know how to best touch their hearts and strengthen your love and friendship in the future.

Prepare for the exercise by taking a few minutes to answer the questions on the following pages. It will be useful for you to have written down your answers before you hear the answers from your family members. Then gather your family and do the exercise with them, using the instructions listed after the questions.

I. What are three of the most memorable experiences you have had with me?

What would your spouse say about you?

A.

B.

C.

What would your children say about you?

A.

B.

C.

What would your extended family—brothers, sisters, parents, in-laws, and so on—say about you?

A.

B.

C.

II. List three to five things that you appreciate most about me.

What would your spouse say about you?

A.

B.

C.

D.

E.

What would your children say about you?

A.

B.

C.

D.

E.

What would your extended family—brothers, sisters, parents, in-laws, and so on—say about you?

A.

B.

C.

D.

E.

III. What do I do to show you that I love you?

What would your spouse say about you?

A.

B.

C.

D.

E.

What would your children say about you?

A.

B.

C.

D.

E.

What would your extended family—brothers, sisters, parents, in-laws, and so on—say about you?

A.

B.

C.

D.

E.

IV. List three to five positive attributes, behaviors, or values that you will remember most about me in the years to come.

What would your spouse say about you?

A.

B.

C.

D.

E.

What would your children say about you?

A.

B.

C.

D.

E.

What would your extended family—brothers, sisters, parents, in-laws, and so on—say about you?

A.

B.

C.

D.

E.

V. List two things that you want me to do more frequently.

What would your spouse say about you?

A.

B.

What would your children say about you?

A.

B.

What would your extended family—brothers, sisters, parents, in-laws, and so on—say about you?

A.

B.

Steps to Doing the "Leveraging Your Strengths" Exercise with Your Family and Others with Whom You Have Personal Relationships

Step 1. *Write each of the five questions on a separate 3 x 5-inch lined index card (or a 4 x 6-inch lined index card).* You should have a set of five cards prepared for every person who will participate. You should also provide each person with a pen or pencil to work with. If you are working with children younger than 8 years old, you may want your spouse to help them to understand the questions and write down their answers.

Questions (one per card):

- What are three of the most memorable experiences you have had with me?
- List three to five things that you appreciate most about me.
- What do I do to show you that I love you?
- List three to five positive attributes, behaviors, or values that you will remember most about me in the years to come.
- List two things that you want me to do more frequently.

Step 2. *Gather your family in a meeting and explain the purpose of the exercise.* Explain that you are very interested in getting their feedback on what you have done well and the types of good memories they have of you. Explain that you are trying to be a better person and to strengthen your relationship with them. In order to strengthen the relationship, you would like to know some of the things you have done in the past that have strengthened it. Explain that you want to make sure that you understand what the members of your family appreciate so that you can do more of it in the future. They should write the answers to the questions as individuals, not as a collective group.

Step 3. *Hand out the cards and ask the members of your family to fill in the answers to the questions.* You may want to leave the room so that they can write without you watching them. Give them plenty of time to write—as long as 5 to 7 minutes for each question. Generally, children will start to lose interest if this exercise goes on for longer than 30 minutes.

Step 4. *Discuss their answers as a group.* We have found that the meeting can be the most fun and enjoyable if you have a discussion right in the meeting in which each person shares his or her ideas. Take one question at a time and go around the room, with each person describing what she or he wrote. This can be a fun and uplifting exercise. Collect the cards after your discussion and explain that you want to review them carefully and try to do more of the things that people have written.

The Value of Creating Future Memories

Your careful review of the positive comments in response to these five simple questions can provide valuable clues to the kind of behavior that will build and forge strong relationships. For example, look at the responses one of our coaching participants gave to the question "What are three of the most memorable experiences you have had with me?"

> Two memories really stand out. First, we had lengthy and deep conversations long distance between Memphis and California before we were married. My second most memorable experience with him is when we drove cross-country to Memphis and he came with a lengthy list of preprinted questions that helped us get to know each other and pass the time on the long driving stretches.

Why do you think this spouse had such wonderful memories of these two events? What do these memories say about what she feels is important? In this particular case, the spouse valued conversations that allowed the two of them to get to know each other. She valued personal and deep conversations, the one-on-one time together, the exploration of what was in each other's mind and heart. She valued the preparation it took to create the questions for the cross-country trip.

What would you guess would help this couple strengthen their relationship? Based on the wife's most memorable experience, what could the husband do to improve the relationship, to capitalize on the strengths of the relationship?

- He could create another list of questions for another cross-country trip or for a cozy conversation by the fireplace. Perhaps he could create a list of questions and see if he and his wife could each guess the correct answer from the other's point of view to see how well they really know each other.
- He could schedule a time just to drive together with his wife and talk about past memories.

With a little effort, our strengths can unlock the door to stronger relationships. We can actually create future memories by building on memorable events and behavior in the past.

What really creates memories? What have others said about the memories and behavior that stand out the most in their minds? An assessment of Family 360 participants reveals an interesting pattern of what creates memories. We found that the five Leveraging Your Strength questions sometimes resulted in surprising answers.

(Remember that, as positive as some of these comments may be, the people who said these things did not necessarily have an ideal relationship. They experienced some of the same frustrations and problems that you may be experiencing.)

1. *Memories of loving care and sensitivity.* We found that spouses and children were profoundly moved when they felt deeply that someone really loved them. The moment at which they felt that love was a memorable, lasting experience that they treasured for years. We also observed that some of the best memories were of situations when the sensitive and caring side of family members and loved ones emerged, particularly when seeing a side that was not always a common experience. Since many of our Family 360 participants are executives and are driven, A-type personalities, they may not always show love and sensitivity toward their families. Frequently, they have to be reminded by their spouses not to treat them as employees when they arrive home from work, or to "check their business face at the door" when they arrive. So situations in which these driven individuals showed a softer, more sensitive side tended to evoke the best memories for their spouse. For example:

- "My greatest memory is when he took such great care of my dad when he fell off the roof and broke his foot. When he heard about it, he drove 160 miles to pick Dad up, took him to a superior hospital, and made sure he had the highest recommended bone specialist."
- "The births of our daughters were memorable thanks to my husband's strength, love, and support."
- From a daughter: "My best memory is when my grandmother died. Even though my mother was sad, she made sure I was always okay. When we were together during the funeral, she hugged me and told me funny stories about my grandma when she was alive. It helped me feel better."
- "My favorite memory of my dad is when my mom gave him a collage of pictures and he cried."

2. ***Memories of simple, thoughtful acts.*** Comments about memories can be brief, even only a few words, but they usually speak volumes. Even the smallest, most insignificant event may have been the most memorable. For example, a parent may say that going to the circus was the most memorable event. A child may say, "Playing basketball after work" or "shopping in the mall with my mother" was the most memorable event. One woman said the strongest memory that built her relationship with her sister was a simple act from years earlier when they were both in high school together: "Way back when I was in high school, my sister gave me a pair of beautiful earrings. They were topaz, and she said she bought them because she thought they matched my eyes and that I would look beautiful in them."

The most memorable experiences cited by children:

- "When we play together."
- "When he helps me with my homework."
- "Jumping on the trampoline."
- "His reading bedtime stories to me when I was young."
- "When she just helps me when I am having hard times."
- "We used to play on the playground and have fun!"
- "Game nights as a kid."

- "Our talks about jobs, politics, movies, and so on."
- "Going to the movies together."
- "Being our coach for biddy ball."
- "Taking me out of school to go fishing."
- "When he taught me to ride my bike."

The most memorable experiences cited by spouses:
- "Calling me from work just to tell me he was thinking about me."
- "Taking me on a business trip and spending time together."
- "He comes home and takes over the responsibilities with the children."
- "I enjoy driving and talking together."
- "Expressing appreciation for the work I have done, both in my job and around the house."

3. *Memories of giving meaningful service.* Many of the activities that were the most memorable involved doing meaningful, service-oriented activities together. Service activities tended to evoke feelings of pride, accomplishment, and goodwill toward others.

- "My best memory is sharing in the care of our dying grandmother over the last 2 years of her life, especially in the final days."
- "When we work together to provide Thanksgiving dinner for the homeless, there is no contention. Everyone has a sense that we are really helping others."
- "Our family went regularly to the retirement home for years and we played games with the residents and just talked to them. We found out about their lives and tried to be their friends. We have vivid memories of serving as a family."

4. *Memories of one-on-one time.* Some of the most memorable experiences were the one-on-one times together, times when two people could just talk—spouses, father and child, mother and child.

- "During the summer we had a special day together, just the two of us. We went to the mall and shopped and just talked. We ate lunch at Sweet

Tomatoes, and her cone broke and she dropped her ice cream and she wiped her finger on my potato. We couldn't stop laughing."
- "All of our MSU baseball and basketball and football game trips with just me and my dad."
- "We play a game of pool every night before bedtime. It's our time to talk and have fun. And sometimes I even beat him."
- "Our daddy-daughter dates. We go get ice cream or go shopping or just play games."

Summary of Leveraging Your Strengths

One important key to closing the gap between where we are and where we want to be is to focus on our strengths. Often we do not understand what others view as our strengths, nor do we realize how valued even small actions can be for our family. We can quickly identify some of our strengths through the Leveraging Your Strengths exercise. We need to understand what we do well and do it more often, with more people, and in more situations:

- If we can understand what attributes and behaviors are most appreciated by others, we can try to exhibit more of those behaviors in order to create a lasting legacy with our loved ones.
- If we can understand how we have created positive memorable experiences for those with whom we have close relationships, we will have some great clues for what to do to achieve lasting memories.
- If we understand our strengths in one area, we can leverage them and apply them in other situations and with other people.
- If we apply our strengths in more areas and with more family members, we will create more uplifting, positive experiences in our families.

Family 360:
Gathering the Data

"The happiest moments of my life have been the few which I have passed at home in the bosom of my family."

—Thomas Jefferson

How to Conduct the Family 360 Survey

THERE ARE SEVERAL ways you can have your family members and others with whom you have personal relationships provide you with feedback through the Family 360 survey. The following seven-step process is the easiest way to conduct a Family 360 survey and is the approach we recommend and coach Family 360 participants to use. We will describe the process in length here in Chapter 7.

Here is an overview of the steps in the Family 360 process:

1. Gather your family in a family council.
2. Write the answer scale on a large piece of paper.
3. Hand out 3 x 5-inch or 4 x 6-inch answer cards.
4. Read Family 360 questions (all 55 questions).
5. Collect the answer cards and calculate scores.
6. Review the best practices section for ideas on how to improve.
7. Develop an action plan with your family.

We strongly recommend that you go through all 55 Family 360 questions with your spouse and children *in one sitting*, rather than break them up into three separate council meetings corresponding to the core, relationship, and growth behaviors.

How Much Time Does the Family 360 Process Take?

- *Steps 1 through 4 will take about 45 to 60 minutes with your entire family.* It takes only a few minutes to explain the purpose of the Family 360 council and set the ground rules. It may take a few minutes to describe the Family 360 survey response scale and how to use it. It should take only about 20 to 25 minutes to run through the list of 55 questions.
- *Steps 5 and 6 will require approximately 2 hours of your own time to do the analysis well.* You will analyze the data you received from your family members and prepare ideas for actions you can take to leverage your strengths and to work on the areas needing improvement. It may take a little longer if you have more family members and thus more numbers to analyze. We recommend that you set aside approximately 2 hours. Approximately 60 minutes will be needed to calculate the average score for each question and assess which questions had the highest score (most positive) and which received the lowest score (most needing attention). We recommend that you then spend another 60 minutes thinking through two or three ideas for things you can do to build on your strengths and improve your weaknesses. The Best Practices Guide in this book can be helpful.
- *Step 7 will require approximately 60 minutes to meet with your family again and discuss their responses and ideas for improving your relationship with the family.* You will want to give them the information on the highest and lowest scores and then develop two or three actions to include in an action plan document.

Let's Discuss Steps 1 through 7 in More Depth

Step 1. *Gather your family for a family council, explain the purpose of the meeting, and set the ground rules.* Plan for this council carefully and thoughtfully. Find a time when all family members or others with whom you have important relationships can be in attendance. Choose a place where disruptions will be minimal and the atmosphere is relaxed. Allow enough time to cover all the planned agenda items as well as any spontaneous topics that may come up.

Write out what you want to say and, perhaps, how you will say it. Then gather your family together and explain how you would like their help to become a better spouse and parent. *The purpose of the Family 360 exercise is to find out how you can be better at strengthening personal relationships, not what your family members can do to be better.* This is an important point. Family members cannot feel that they are the ones who are under the microscope here—you are. Describe how you would like their honest and candid evaluation of some of your behaviors. Tell them that you sincerely want their help. Apologize if you have not exhibited proper behavior in the past. This is a very important step in establishing your sincerity.

Thank everyone for attending and set the ground rules for the discussion. Everyone should participate. No one should criticize, be defensive, or make fun of others' comments or suggestions. The Family 360 council is supposed to be upbeat and constructive. You want their honest and candid feedback as well as their help in developing an action plan.

Step 2. *Write the answer scale on a large piece of paper or a paper pad on an easel.* For example, write the following seven responses on a large piece of paper where they are visible to everyone in the room. You will want to define what each response means. (The Family 360 survey questions are worded so that someone as young as 10 years old can answer them. For those younger than 10, we recommend that a spouse assist the child in understanding and answering the questions. Children as young as 7 or 8 can understand most of the concepts in the survey.)

Needs Significant Attention	Needs Some Attention	Almost Acceptable	Acceptable	More than Acceptable	Strength	Significant Strength
1	2	3	4	5	6	7

Explain the following: "As I read the questions, I will want you to write down how you feel about my behavior in this area.

121

- "Write down 1 if my behavior needs significant attention. This is an area where you want me to really improve. You may feel that I really need to work to improve.
- "Write down 7 if you think this is one of my biggest strengths. You feel that it is one of my best behaviors, and you appreciate it.
- "Or write down 4, acceptable, if my behavior in this area is fine, okay, or acceptable. It is neither a strength nor an area needing improvement.
- "Or you can write another number response if the behavior needs some attention (2), is almost acceptable (3), is more than acceptable (5), or is a strength, but not a significant strength (6)."

You can further define the other areas if you think they need more clarification. For young children, you can draw a smiling face on the top of the 7 and a frowning face on the top of the 1 to signify happy behavior and sad behavior.

Step 3. *Hand out 3 x 5-inch or 4 x 6-inch cards.* (You may also choose to distribute copies of the complete survey in Appendix A, but the card method described below is an easy way to gather the data from the questions.) The cards should have lines and be numbered, the first card from 1 through 17, the second card from 18 through 40, and the third card from 41 through 55. It is better if you write the numbers on the card yourself, perhaps drawing a blank space after each number, such as the following:

CARD #1: *Core Behaviors*

1. _____	10. _____
2. _____	11. _____
3. _____	12. _____
4. _____	13. _____
5. _____	14. _____
6. _____	15. _____
7. _____	16. _____
8. _____	17. _____
9. _____	

CARD #2: *Relationship Behaviors*

18. _____	27. _____	36. _____
19. _____	28. _____	37. _____
20. _____	29. _____	38. _____
21. _____	30. _____	39. _____
22. _____	31. _____	40. _____
23. _____	32. _____	
24. _____	33. _____	
25. _____	34. _____	
26. _____	35. _____	

CARD #3: *Growth Behaviors*

41. _____	50. _____
42. _____	51. _____
43. _____	52. _____
44. _____	53. _____
45. _____	54. _____
46. _____	55. _____
47. _____	
48. _____	
49. _____	

Hand out pencils or pens. Describe the exercise you are about to have them do with you. You may want to run through a practice question to see how they will respond. Tell them that you will be collecting the cards at the end so that you can see their answers. Once you see how they have evaluated you, you will discuss with them how you can improve.

Step 4. *Read them the core behavior, relationship behavior, and growth behavior questions contained in Appendix A.* Read the questions slowly and give your family members an opportunity to write down the number that corresponds with their opinion of your behavior.

Step 5. *Collect the cards and calculate the scores.* (If you use the written survey in Appendix A, collect the copies of the survey.) Thank your family members for their participation. Collect the cards and begin the analysis by averaging the responses with a calculator. For example, if you have a spouse and three children, you would have received four scores for Question 1, such as 4, 4, 3, 7.

Add up the scores (in this case, the total is 18) and divide by the number of people who responded (in this case, 4) for the average score (in this case, 4.5). Write down the average score next to the question on the Calculation Form/Action Plan in Appendix B of this book.

Important:

Make this process as simple as possible. Focus on only a few things. You can't expect to do something about everything all at once. Once you know your three to five lowest average scores, you will know what your family and others with whom you have personal relationships would like you to improve. And if you also know your three to five highest average scores, you will know what you can leverage as your strengths.

Step 6. *Review the best practices section and develop some ideas about how to improve.* For example, if you have low scores in a communication area, review the best practices that cover the area where you have the low scores. Try to identify an activity that would be enjoyable and would fit with your family culture. Write down a few notes about each idea on a piece of paper in order to have something to discuss with your family. Remember that these are just ideas that you want to share with your family. The discussion you have with your family in Step 7 will help you identify and finalize the actions that you will want to take. You may find that your family members have ideas that fit your and your family's needs even better than the ideas from the Best Practices Guide.

Step 7. *Develop an action plan with your family.* In preparation for discussing the survey results with your family, write your three to five lowest scores and your three to five highest scores, along with the corresponding questions, on a large piece of paper. You may decide to share the data from all of the questions. This would be particularly helpful if you are sharing the data with just your spouse. However, if you are sharing the information with children, we find that it is not necessary to show all the data, particularly if there are younger family members who may not be able to sit through the discussion. It is more helpful to focus on improving areas that need attention and leveraging your strengths in areas where you already do well.

Bring your family together again. Thank them sincerely for their candid responses to the questions. Tell them that you have found the information very helpful and that you hope to work on a few things to become a better spouse and parent.

Start with the positive scores. Tell them that you want to start with the positive scores in order to find out if there is more you could do to build on your strengths. Read each of the highest-scoring questions in its entirety and then tell your family the average score that you received on that question. For example, you may write the following on a large piece of paper:

Highest-Scoring Questions (Most Positive)
11. Works hard to provide food and a home for the family. *Score: 7.0*
15. Recognizes and respects spouse. *Score: 6.5*
35. Spends time with the children when they need help. *Score: 6.5*
36. Participates in the children's important events and activities. *Score: 6.2*
53. Helps family members improve their talents. *Score: 6.2*

Then continue with your lowest scores. Let your family know that you would like to improve in the areas where you had low scores. For example,

Lowest-Scoring Questions (Need Attention)
1. Is patient with family members. *Score: 3.0*
3. Takes time to have personal conversations. *Score: 3.2*
10. Solves problems without getting angry or keeping silent. *Score: 3.2*
19. Shows love by the things he or she does. *Score: 3.5*
21. Uses a kind voice when speaking. *Score: 3.7*

Personal Preparation

The Family 360 asks questions about the three pillars of effective behaviors for personal and family relationships: core behaviors (Chapter 8), relationship behaviors (Chapter 9), and growth behaviors (Chapter 10). These constitute the heart of Family 360 and the main process for gathering feedback on your behavior. Each of the three chapters is designed to prepare you for the Family 360 and identify ways to improve your behavior and is organized in the following way:

- *Family 360 survey tool.* You will have the opportunity to assess your own behavior prior to gathering data from your family.
- *The big idea.* We will describe the most frequently cited solution and how individuals and families have used this "big idea" to strengthen their personal and family relationships. The big ideas are different in each of the three chapters: Chapter 8 will describe the big idea for developing core behaviors, Chapter 9 the big idea for developing relationship behaviors, and Chapter 10 the big idea for developing growth behaviors.
- *Solutions from the Best Practices Guide.* Over the last 10 years we have spoken with many busy individuals just like you as we have coached people in work/life balance practices. These people have had some wonderful ideas about how to repair, build, and strengthen personal and family relationships. We have included in each chapter a summary of best practices that people have used to develop specific behaviors. The purpose of the Best Practices Guide is to provide the reader with a sampling of great ideas that he or she can adopt or modify for personal use. The Best Practices Guide can serve as a valuable reference tool as you work to develop an action plan for strengthening your personal and family relationships.

In order to help you sort through some of these actions and choose the ones you would like to try, we have divided them into four categories:

1. *Best practice.* These are the actions that busy people mentioned as having a high positive impact on personal and family relationships. In our survey research, at least 15 percent or more of our respondents cited these practices as being very helpful.

2. *High travel solution.* These are the actions that busy people said made a difference for them when they have high travel demands at work. They implemented these practices in order to maintain strong relationships with their families, despite spending a significant amount of time away from them.

3. *Spouse focused.* These actions are specifically mentioned as having a positive impact on the relationship with a spouse.

4. *Children focused.* These actions are specifically mentioned as having a positive impact on the relationship with children.

For example, under "Communication and Listening," you will find the following action item:

Communication and Listening				
Best Practice	**High Travel Solution**	**Spouse Focused**	**Children Focused**	**Action Item**
*	*		*	Learn one new thing about your spouse or your child's day. Ask questions such as, "What was your best experience during the day?" "What was the most interesting thing you learned today?" "What was the most frustrating part of your day?" Use these questions when traveling and phoning home.

The action of asking for a best experience of the day from a spouse and children was mentioned as a best practice. Those who spent a great deal of time away from their family used it most often to stay in touch. It is specifically focused on building a relationship with children. So three of the four categories were marked with an asterisk.

As you review the best practices sections of this book, you may want to use these categories to quickly identify actions that make sense for you and your situation. For example, if you travel frequently, you may want to skim down the column "High Travel Solution." Or, if you are looking for something to strengthen your relationship with your child, you might look for an action that is both a "Best Practice" *and* "Children Focused."

Creation of an action plan. We will describe how to incorporate your feedback into an action plan in Chapter 8.

Core Behaviors

"Communication is a skill that you can learn. It's like riding a bicycle or typing. If you're willing to work at it, you can rapidly improve the quality of every part of your life."

—Brian Tracy

Family 360 Survey Tool for Core Behaviors: Listening, Communicating, Problem Solving, Support, Respect

CORE BEHAVIORS are the behaviors that are fundamental to good personal and family relationships. Along with the basic skills of communication, listening, and problem solving, core behaviors include being sensitive to and respecting other members of the family.

A major oil company in the Far East conducted a week-long, off-site development program for its executives. The wives of the male executives were invited to attend. During one session of the program, the executives and their wives participated in a retreat to talk about work/life issues. They discussed their work goals and the challenges they faced, and they talked about how they could maintain a relationship as a couple, despite a busy work schedule. The program was structured to provide ample time for problem solving as a couple —to come up with specific actions to address the concerns each partner raised.

At the end of the program, the instructor handed out evaluation sheets on the entire week's program. The work/life discussion was rated *by the executives* as the best day of the program. The reason? The executives and their wives had a chance to just talk and listen to each other. The program provided them with a forum where they could discuss and communicate as a group on an important issue and then to communicate and problem-solve privately as couples about important things that they would not normally take the time to discuss.

Given our busy lives, we often find that we may think we are listening and communicating, but we are not. We get caught up in accomplishing things and do not pay attention to those around us.

- "I started out as a good listener, but then I had a family and our family began to grow. There were so many things that took my attention. I found I would be talking to family members 'on the fly'—while I was doing other things, such as making dinner or doing the laundry. I would be doing things while I tried to talk to them. I was not consciously aware of the habit until my youngest son, David, said, 'You're not listening to me.' I realized I had gotten out of the habit of making eye contact. I was not even aware of the problem."
- "Our children say 'Mom' or 'Dad' three times and then automatically assume that we are not listening. We may be listening, but we are not necessarily paying attention to them. We can't really listen and do multitasking at the same time."

An executive described an experience he had had early in his career that demonstrated his lack of these important core behaviors.

I climbed the career ladder fairly quickly, and at a young age I was given access to many corporate perks of senior management. When I was about 30, I was directly involved with the company's senior management team and was used worldwide to help create effective management teams. On one occasion, I was doing consulting work with the Canadian management team. During the middle of the off-site meeting, I received a call from the chairman of the company, who asked to meet with me as soon as possible. The corporate jet had already been sent to bring me back to our Chicago headquarters. The jet was empty except for the pilots and me. When I landed, a stretch limo met me at the company hangar. During the 30-minute ride to headquarters, I just basked in the luxury of the moment—I served myself something to drink from the limo bar, watched a little of *Oprah* on the TV, and then used the limo phone to call my wife to share the events of the day and to gloat a bit. After I described the lavish way I was being treated, there was a pause on the other end of the phone—a long pause. And then my wife finally asked, "So . . . when are you going to come home and change a diaper?"

The message went right to my heart. I had forgotten what was truly important. I was not very respectful of my wife and the difficult challenge she had during the day, and I was certainly not listening to her difficulties and finding out how I could be more supportive. It was one of many wake-up calls I've received over the years. Luckily my wife has a sense of humor—as a present she gave me a toy limo (a tiny toy car, I might add) to fulfill my need and put in perspective what is truly important.

Prior to giving the Family 360 survey to your family, take a few minutes and evaluate yourself. How are you doing on these core behaviors? Look through the following list of 17 questions and score yourself on how well you exhibit the core behaviors. Use your self-scored highs to identify strengths and your lows to identify areas for improvement and look through the Best Practices Guide for ideas on how to leverage your strengths and improve on areas that need attention. Then give the Family 360 exercise to your family and compare your self-assessment scores with those of your family members.

FAMILY 360 SURVEY: *Core Behavior Questions*

Communication and Listening							
	Needs Significant Attention	Needs Some Attention	Almost Acceptable	Acceptable	More than Acceptable	Strength	Significant Strength
1. Is patient with family members	○	○	○	○	○	○	○

Family 360

Core Behavior Questions/Communication and Listening (*continued*)

	Needs Significant Attention	Needs Some Attention	Almost Acceptable	Acceptable	More than Acceptable	Strength	Significant Strength
2. Openly talks about important things	O	O	O	O	O	O	O
3. Takes time to have personal conversations	O	O	O	O	O	O	O
4 Listens to what others have to say	O	O	O	O	O	O	O
5. Pays attention to personal feelings when communicating	O	O	O	O	O	O	O
6. Openly talks about what he or she has learned from his or her mistakes	O	O	O	O	O	O	O
7. Is fair and consistent with family members	O	O	O	O	O	O	O
Problem Solving							
8. Seeks fair solutions to problems	O	O	O	O	O	O	O
9. Helps resolve disagreements to everyone's satisfaction	O	O	O	O	O	O	O

Core Behavior Questions/Problem Solving (*continued*)

	Needs Significant Attention	Needs Some Attention	Almost Acceptable	Acceptable	More than Acceptable	Strength	Significant Strength
10. Solves problems without getting angry or keeping silent	O	O	O	O	O	O	O
Support							
11. Works hard to provide food and a home for the family	O	O	O	O	O	O	O
12. Makes sure that all family members' needs are met	O	O	O	O	O	O	O
13. Helps family members feel safe and secure at home	O	O	O	O	O	O	O
Equal Partnership and Respect							
14. Recognizes and respects spouse's role in the home	O	O	O	O	O	O	O
15. Recognizes and respects spouse's job role	O	O	O	O	O	O	O
16. Shares fairly in rearing children	O	O	O	O	O	O	O
17. Shares home chores fairly	O	O	O	O	O	O	O

Big Idea 1: Hold a Regular Family Council

"Big ideas" are included in each of the next three chapters. We have selected these ideas from the hundreds of ideas that we have seen busy people use. They are the ideas that seem to be the most common and useful ideas of Family 360 participants. A big idea is an idea that, in our assessment, warrants imitation by everyone. It is one of the few best practices that can be adapted for use by everyone, with effective results.

Most families today are inundated with things to do, places to go, and activities in which to participate. Many of these families revel in their busyness. They like the family to participate in many activities in order to expand their horizons, develop their talents, and explore new interests. As a result, many family members circle in different orbits—they travel with different schedules, have competing and conflicting commitments, and can lead fairly chaotic lives.

A family council is an administrative tool that helps a family run smoothly, cooperatively, and as a close unit. (In Chapter 9, we will cover a big idea for relationship behaviors: the family night. A family night is the cousin of the family council and focuses more on building and improving the relationships within the family. Family councils help to administer the communication needs of the family unit, while the family night ministers to the relationship needs of the family unit.)

The Purpose of a Family Council

The purpose of a family council is to allow family members to counsel each other. They are designed to encourage open and honest communication on issues of concern within the family. These concerns can include how to better coordinate family activities and calendars, how to help the family run smoothly, how to implement consistent rules and discipline, and how to bring more fun and service into the family. Family councils work whether the family consists of two people or ten people, as noted by families who have taken the approach:

- "Family councils are going well. We are not systematic yet, but the conversations are going well. I use them as a way to facilitate conversations between my wife and me. The dialogue is a two-way street."

- "One of the things that has come out of our family councils is a heightened sensitivity to each other and to the need for all of us to be more proactive. We have all recognized the need to build more focused family time into our schedules, especially on the weekend. We are now more purposeful in doing things with the family."

- "With the Family Council we have more structure around finding time for ourselves. We build time into our schedules for each other and for the family. I have three children, ages 6, 4, and 1. I am trying to be more sensitive with our children and their needs, and how we can build more time into our schedule for them. What we do today may leave impressions with them for future years."

- "Family councils allow everyone to participate in decision making for the family. They work well whether we are planning our summer vacation or what we are doing on the weekend."

The Key Components of a Family Council

Planning/coordination of weekly activities. The meeting is an opportunity to coordinate calendars, to identify conflicts, and to discuss ways to help one another participate in various activities. Family calendars can be coordinated with work calendars. Rides and times of dinner can be coordinated and agreed upon.

Planning/coordination of monthly/annual activities. In addition to being useful for planning and organizing weekly activities, the meeting is an opportunity to plan activities to do as a family unit during the year. It is an ideal time to brainstorm and discuss weekend trips, holiday adventures, or summer or winter vacation plans.

Coordinating family chores. Every family needs to operate smoothly. Like any business, the family needs to have coordinated jobs and tasks. Everyone in the family needs to be able to make a contribution to helping the family run smoothly, without placing the burden on any one person. Council meetings are an ideal forum to discuss chores and develop chore charts, plan incentives and rewards for those who contribute to the family, and plan allowances for family members.

Establishing family discipline. Every family operates by a set of expectations and behavior standards. Most of the time, these standards are the expected norm—they are not written down or discussed. Unfortunately, even a family needs to discuss and develop its own standards of behavior and performance and what is expected from family members. Behavioral expectations should be agreed upon and written down. Discipline for not meeting the standards of behavior should also be discussed and agreed upon. (We do not propose to deal with the subject of family rules and discipline in this book—there are numerous approaches to creating discipline. The idea of a family council underscores the need to have an open discussion and agreement on the type of rules and discipline that the family will utilize.)

How to Hold a Family Council: The Agenda

Step 1. *Set aside a specific time once a week, preferably at the beginning of the week.* Everyone should be aware of the time, location, and purpose of the meeting. Make sure that there is a treat or dessert for after the meeting in order to encourage attendance.

Step 2. *Develop a brief agenda of topics you would like the family to discuss.* You may want to consider developing the agenda for subsequent council meetings at the very first meeting. Explain that the family council will be a way in which everyone can have input into family decisions—vacation plans, activities, family discipline, and so on. Ask the family members to create a list of things that they would like to discuss in upcoming meetings.

Step 3. *Coordinate calendars for the coming week.* Bring out your work and family calendars and discuss the activities for each day. Keep a family calendar, with all the main activities of all family members coordinated, posted in a prominent location. Discuss and resolve conflicts, coordinate rides, and discuss any unplanned activities. Be sure to include special occasions, such as birthdays, special sports events, recitals, anniversaries, and so on, in the discussion.

Step 4. *Plan one fun family activity for the week.* This could be a simple activity that everyone participates in together. It could be as simple as a Friday night movie, a game night, an out-to-dinner night, an early morning basketball game with the kids, or a trip to the ice cream shop.

Step 5. *Discuss other issues of concern.* This would be the ideal time to gather information and plan vacations and special family outings. This is also the time to discuss any concerns about behaviors, discipline, or family rules. Make sure you deal with these issues in a positive way. No one will want to come to the next council meeting if people feel that it is Mom or Dad's opportunity to rail at the other members of the family.

Step 6. *Have a treat.* This could be as simple as breaking out the Oreo cookies and milk or building your own ice cream sundaes.

Critical Success Factors for the Family Council

What will make the family council work best? Here is some advice from those who have participated in these councils:

1. *Keep the family council meeting an upbeat experience.* Do not allow the council to deteriorate into a gripe session. The council should be constructive and collaborative. Anger and impatience should not surface during the discussion. Hidden agendas can quickly backfire and should be kept to a minimum. For example, a parent may want to complain about the children's scattering their dishes around the kitchen and leaving the mess for the parents to clean up. The council would backfire if the children felt that the meeting was an excuse to dump on them or to complain about their behavior. A better approach would be to work on the positive side of the problem behavior: "How can we have a home that is neat and clean and that everyone feels good about living in?" If negative comments begin to enter into the discussion, ask to take the discussion "off-line," meaning, "The issue is important and we want to discuss it, but let's talk about this off to the side."

2. *Councils should include full participation by every member of the family.* They should not be viewed as being driven by one person or by the parents. There should be equal say, open discussion and participation, and candid problem solving. No ideas are stupid or lack merit. All members should feel that their opinion is valued and important to the discussion. Criticism of ideas and comments should be kept to a minimum. Even the youngest member should feel that his or her opinions are valuable.

3. *Family councils should end with at least one action item for family members to implement during the coming weeks.* Decisions that cannot be made during the meeting or on which there is a difference of opinion should be deferred to the next meeting. Council meetings should result in a specific outcome and activity that can be followed up in subsequent council meetings.

4. *Family councils should be an example of patient problem solving.* Parents should go into the session with a firm resolve not to let contention or anger enter into the discussion. They should commit to help each other, not become impatient, sarcastic, or critical.

5. *Family councils should be held regularly, even if they last for only 10 minutes.* Councils work best if they become a habit and an expected way of coordinating activities and planning. We have found that a simple dessert after the council meeting is a good way to encourage participation and to help everyone look forward to the meeting.

Solutions from the Best Practices Guide

The following actions come from the many people we have worked with over the years and the descriptions they have given of ways in which they built and strengthened their personal relationships. In essence, these actions have been tested in real life and may prove helpful for you. (A full description of how to make the most effective use of the Best Practices Guide is in Chapter 7.)

Best Practice	High Travel Solution	Spouse Focused	Children Focused	Action Item
				Communication and Listening
		*	*	Go for a walk with your spouse or a child once each day, even if it is just around the block or to the end of the driveway. Spend the few minutes together asking the other person questions about her or his day and experiences, or just talking about whatever she or he wants to talk about.
*	*		*	Provide your children and your spouse with ready access to you. Give family members a phone number where you can be reached at work. Consider establishing an 800 phone number for those living away from home or providing cell phones so that the children can stay in touch.
*			*	Phone home. Call home during your workday to find out about your children's day at school. Encourage your children to contact you at work when appropriate.
*	*		*	Learn one new thing about your spouse or your child's day. Ask questions such as, "What was your best experience during the day?" "What was the most interesting thing you learned today?" "What was the most frustrating part of your day?" Use these questions when traveling and phoning home.
			*	Stimulate communication during dinner. Put preselected questions on (or under) the dinner plates of family members. One day the questions may focus on imaginative topics, the next time on current events, another time on individual interests, and so on.
			*	During dinner, go around the table and take turns telling the funniest thing that happened all day long. Or, tell one thing that was learned during the day.
			*	Help set goals. Talk with a child about her or his goals for the coming week or month. Post the goals on a goal chart. The beginning of the school year is a good time to talk about and establish goals for the coming year.

Communication and Listening (*continued*)

Best Practice	High Travel Solution	Spouse Focused	Children Focused	Action Item
			*	Involve children in candid value discussions using real-life scenarios. Teach them about values by talking to them about real-life examples from home, from school, in the community, or at work. Ask them about the most difficult problem they have faced at school and how they resolved the problem.
*			*	Talk about the dilemmas, disagreements, and difficulties you face at work and ask them how they would resolve the real problems. Use real-life examples of disagreements, challenges, or ethical choices that you have experienced. Ask them how they would resolve the problem; then share how you handled the situation.
			*	Discuss how you have mishandled real-life problems at work or at school. Ask your children or your spouse what they think you should have done differently.
*				Use your commute time to mentally prepare for being home. Listen to uplifting or classical music during your drive home to get your mind in the proper spirit. Imagine facing the worst situation possible when you walk through the door and role-play in your mind how you will calmly handle the situation.
*				Prepare for being home by pulling into the garage and spending a few minutes thinking about how you will react to your spouse and your children when you enter the home. Think of the worst situation you may face and role-play how you will handle the situation.
*	*		*	Buy a speakerphone for your home. When you are out of town, call home and talk with the entire family on the speakerphone. If you are out of town for an extended length of time or working late, these joint calls can be used to avoid missing regularly scheduled family times such as family council or family game night.
			*	Call home and use the speakerphone to read stories, tell jokes, or interview your family members.

Communication and Listening (*continued*)

Best Practice	High Travel Solution	Spouse Focused	Children Focused	Action Item
*	*		*	Videotape yourself reading bedtime stories or talking to your family prior to leaving on an extended business trip.
	*		*	Videotape messages for those special occasions —birthdays, sports events, performances, holidays, big tests at school, braces coming off, going for a driver's license, and so on—when you will be absent from the family.
	*		*	When you are away from home, select one child each night and have a personal one-on-one phone conversation with that child.
	*		*	When you are on the road, use the fax machine. Have children fax their homework or assignments to you so that you can be part of helping them, even though you are absent.
*	*	*	*	Use email to stay in touch with family members when you are out of town. Send a message every morning you are away. Compliment the achievements of the family, talk about activities at work, tell a joke you heard that day, and so on.
		*	*	Keep a pad of paper and envelopes in your briefcase or pocketbook. Write a short, personal weekly letter to each family member, even when you are not traveling.
		*	*	Take advantage of the many small moments you have with a spouse or a child. Create communication opportunities while waiting in line, riding in the car, working in the yard, or doing the dishes.
		*	*	Create a message center in your home where the entire family can easily view and place messages, calendars, and announcements. Use the message center to post announcements about activities that involve family members, calendars with dates and times for family members' events, Post-it notes for messages to family members, and other planning items.

Communication and Listening (*continued*)

Best Practice	High Travel Solution	Spouse Focused	Children Focused	Action Item
	*	*		Establish a set time each day to speak with your spouse or your children, even if for only a few minutes.
	*	*	*	Communicate with your children or spouse by writing short notes and hiding them in lunch bags, posting them on the mirror, putting them in shoes, and so on.
		*	*	Involve a family coach. To audit your family conversations, you may want to enlist the aid of another family member—either a spouse or an older child. This person can observe your conversations and give you private feedback on communication problems, such as the number of times you interrupt a conversation, how frequently you let yourself become distracted during a conversation, how frequently you push your own point of view rather than listen, and how frequently you display unhelpful communication styles—anger, sarcasm, impatience, and so on.
		*	*	Create a family web site and include family pictures, letters, or the latest news for all the family members to read and see.
*		*	*	Focus on the family when you are at home and select specific days when you dedicate your time after work exclusively to the family. Rather than get involved in work email and phone calls, try to leave the office at the office and dedicate most of your evening time to prime family relationships. If necessary, pressing work can be performed after children have gone to bed or early in the mornings.
			*	Establish a bedtime ritual of communicating with your spouse or your children. Ask them to reflect on the day and ask, "What did you do right today?" Or, "How were you helpful to someone else?" Or, "What was the most enjoyable part of the day?" If family members have a difficult time expressing their feelings, you can ask them how they feel about the day: "Is this a

Communication and Listening (*continued*)

Best Practice	High Travel Solution	Spouse Focused	Children Focused	Action Item
				one-, two-, or three-smile day or a one-, two-, or three-frown day?" "On a scale of 1 to 10, with 10 being very happy and 1 being very sad, how did you feel today? Why?"
*		*	*	Write letters of encouragement and love prior to big events. Give them as gifts to family members. For example, write a letter to your daughter on her 16th birthday, when she goes to college, when she decides to get married, and so on. Write a letter to your spouse on your anniversary, when he or she accomplishes a major project at work, when your last child leaves home, and so on. Keep copies of these letters for your own files or journal.
			*	Strengthen your listening abilities by playing "Recollection." During a 5-minute period of time, see how many questions you can ask in rapid sequence to keep a conversation going. Listen to the answers from another family member. After 5 minutes of conversation, try to recall and review all the details of what you heard. Have other family members add to your list.
			*	Implement "Rewind and Replay." Recognize when you are using an impatient tone of voice. When you find yourself doing so, stop and say, "I'm sorry. That's not what I meant to say" or "Let's start over." Then repeat your statement, but this time with a more patient tone of voice.
			*	Enlist the help of a patience coach, such as your spouse. Ask him or her to give you a predetermined, yet subtle sign when he or she observes your patience level waning or your voice rising. A predetermined movement of the hand or fingers, a fake cough, or a catchy phrase such as "Watch your altitude" could be the signal from the coach that you are doing something wrong or that your voice is getting angry. This is particularly helpful when you are interacting with family members or children.

Communication and Listening (*continued*)

Best Practice	High Travel Solution	Spouse Focused	Children Focused	Action Item
			*	Motivate yourself to eliminate poor listening and problem-solving behaviors. For example, if impatience is something you are trying to improve, offer $10 each time you are caught raising your voice or showing a lack of patience. Describe and agree upon the specific behavior you are trying to extinguish. The money could be given to the individual being affected, or it could be put into a jar to fund a family activity.
				Create a "time-out" flag. Have a small colored flag readily available that can be raised or placed in a visible stand when a family member is feeling uncomfortable with the tone or intensity of a conversation. When someone raises the flag, it means that everyone should take a 30-second break in the conversation. Have the person who raised the flag relate why she or he feels uncomfortable, along with a positive statement about the person who was "flagged." The discussion can take place some time after the heat of the moment has passed.
*			*	Utilize driving time to improve communications. Invite a spouse or child to accompany you on an errand or a short trip. Combine your errand with one of his or hers. Driving time, when there are few distractions, can provide many opportunities to talk openly and in private.
		*	*	Establish regular times for communicating with family members. Set aside time, perhaps every Sunday morning or at bedtime, to spend 10 minutes one-on-one to discuss their personal goals, ambitions, talents, or interests. You may consider asking them how you can improve your relationship with them and report on your efforts during the next meeting.
*			*	Establish a bedtime ritual of reading stories to your children, rubbing their back, or just talking in the dark. Use the time to ask about their friends, their goals, their happy moments during the day, and so on.

Communication and Listening (*continued*)

Best Practice	High Travel Solution	Spouse Focused	Children Focused	Action Item
		*	*	Use cleanup time after dinner to talk together. Use the time while you are cleaning up to talk about the activities of the day.
*			*	If you have young children, set a timer for 10 minutes and do chores, clean a room, or do other cleanup activities while you try to beat the buzzer. Talk and ask questions while you are hurrying to get the chore done before the buzzer goes off.
*		*	*	Have a regular family game night, even if there are only two people. Play favorite active and fun games, such as Guesstures, Apples to Apples, Pictionary, Charades, Cranium, or chess.
	*	*	*	Establish a set time each day to have dinner, when everyone is expected to be home. If you are traveling, call home during that time.
*		*		Set aside time to counsel with your spouse. This is a time to talk about the family, how individual family members are doing, what you could do to help strengthen individual family members, and how to improve the atmosphere in the home. This is also a good time to talk about your primary relationship with each other and to ask how to strengthen your relationship, how to treat each other in front of the children, how to be more effective in resolving problems, how you can improve the example you are setting in the home, and so on.
		*	*	Make a commitment to not watch TV after work for a set period of time (e.g., 1 week) and spend the time with family members—helping them with homework, and so on.
*		*	*	After discussion with your family, ask them to commit to unplugging the TV for at least 1 week. Spend the extra time playing games, working on fun projects, baking, visiting friends, and so on.
			*	Create a central point in the home for all homework and computer activities. Mom and Dad can do bills, do work emails, help with homework, and so on, and children can draw, do homework, work on the computer, and so on.

Communication and Listening (*continued*)

Best Practice	High Travel Solution	Spouse Focused	Children Focused	Action Item
			*	Cut out articles from the *Wall Street Journal* or some local newspaper on politics, international events, editorial cartoons or letters, and so on. Bring the articles to dinner and have each member of the family read the articles and discuss the pros and cons of their position.
			*	Conduct a family "press conference" and ask questions of a family member as a reporter would. Pick a current event and ask this family member what he or she would do in this situation. For example, designate one as the president of the United States and ask questions about his or her strategy for fighting terrorism. Or designate one as the president of Sudan and ask how she or he would combat hunger in the country. You can also do a "press conference lite" with questions about their own hobbies and activities.

Problem Solving

Best Practice	High Travel Solution	Spouse Focused	Children Focused	Action Item
*				When a problem occurs in the family, openly discuss the natural outcomes of certain behaviors. For example, in your family council, talk about what happens when someone lies to another person—have the members of your family describe the natural consequences, how people feel, and how trust within the family is eroded. Talk about effective ways to solve the problem and ways that are not effective. Discuss the natural consequences of each approach.
*			*	Involve children in establishing family rules and in setting consequences and discipline for breaking family rules and expectations. Write your decisions down and display them in a prominent location.

Problem Solving (*continued*)

Best Practice	High Travel Solution	Spouse Focused	Children Focused	Action Item
			*	Teach the laws of nature and how they apply to personal relationships. For example, give children responsibility for growing a garden or taking care of the lawn. Discuss the natural principles involved in growing a garden and compare them to those involved in growing relationships.
*			*	Play "What Would You Do?" All families and individuals experience unexpected, as well as planned, change. Develop the ability to adapt to change and to see the positive in difficult situations. Identify various stressful scenarios in the newspaper, from news programs, or from people, friends, and families that you know. Discuss those situations as though they had happened to your family. Pretend that you are facing the situations that you have identified. You might ask, "What would we do if one of our family members was seriously injured in an accident? If the house caught fire? If Dad or Mom lost a job? If Mom became ill? If we had to move?" Take each scenario and identify changes that would take place for each individual. Discuss possible adjustments that would have to be made. Talk about the changes that would be possible and the success that the family would have in adapting to the situation. As you talk about the various scenarios and changes that the family could make, also talk about the family's ability to adapt. Build confidence in being able to handle changes. Ask what positive outcomes could come out of potentially tragic events.
*			*	Develop and discuss the types of decisions that family members can make in advance and why. For example, they can decide in advance to always wear their seat belt, not smoke, be honest, help someone in need, do their home-work when they first arrive home, study for a test days before the test, and so on.
		*	*	Create a sticker chart that records and recognizes those who successfully resolve problems in a peaceful, amicable way and display it in a

Problem Solving (*continued*)

Best Practice	High Travel Solution	Spouse Focused	Children Focused	Action Item
				prominent location. The chart should include Mom and Dad as well as the children. Recognize those who have consistently resolved problems by having them choose where to go to eat out as a family or what movie to see.
			*	Teach each other how to learn from mistakes. Identify mistakes that people have made, from the newspaper, current events, television, personal knowledge, or other sources. Ask what could be learned from the mistake and how that new knowledge can be applied to future situations.
		*		Keep a patience journal. For a specified period of time, observe your interactions with family members with whom you are impatient. Record your observations by writing your feelings and thoughts about your interactions and what would help improve your interactions. At the end of the time period, read your entries in the journal and look for patterns of behavior that you want to change. Consider sharing some of your journal entries with the person with whom you are impatient and make specific commitments to the person to improve.
				Hold a brainstorming session with the family to address a specific family problem. Encourage all family members to participate. Have a rule that no idea presented is criticized or ridiculed. Try to have everyone be creative and "think outside the box." Do not take the time to discuss the details of the suggestions at this stage. List all suggestions on pieces of paper and tape them to the wall or write them on a large pad of paper. After exhausting all ideas, go back and begin evaluating each suggestion, looking for reasonableness, merit, and value in creating an ultimate solution.
			*	When there are arguments or disagreements between children, meet as a family council and have the arguments sung by the opposing parties. Do the singing in good humor. If necessary, help the children make up the words to a familiar tune. Tunes should also include words on how to solve the problem.

Problem Solving (*continued*)

Best Practice	High Travel Solution	Spouse Focused	Children Focused	Action Item
		*		Establish the practice of not talking about the solutions to a problem until each of the two disagreeing parties can successfully restate the position of the other person.
			*	Establish a "peacemaker award." Give the award to the person who tries to resolve problems and maintain a spirit of peace in the home, without arguing or escalating problems.
		*		Implement an adult "time-out." Acknowledge that at times parents and adults need to go on a time-out just as children do. If you become angry during a disagreement, consider visibly putting yourself on a time-out.
*		*	*	Be a role model for apologizing when needed. Recognize the power of sincerely apologizing to your family members when you have offended someone or have acted inappropriately. Some of the sweetest moments of conversations and reconciliations can come after a humble apology to a child or a spouse.

				Support
Best Practice	High Travel Solution	Spouse Focused	Children Focused	Action Item
		*	*	Make a written statement of your personal commitment to support and help your family and review it with your family regularly.
*			*	Involve all family members in the effort to support the home and family. For example, play "Beat the Buzzer." Identify a room that needs to be cleaned or a particular chore that needs to be performed. Have the family members determine how long they feel the task should take to complete. Set a buzzer or timer for the determined amount of time. Everyone then frantically races the buzzer to complete the task. If the chore or task is completed before the buzzer sounds, a small reward can be given. Keep the time period relatively short—10 to 15 minutes.

Support (*continued*)

Best Practice	High Travel Solution	Spouse Focused	Children Focused	Action Item
		*	*	Create a chore chart to share the home chores. There are many ways to distribute chores. For example, you can create a total list of chores and have each child, starting with the youngest, select a chore and put it on her or his chart for the week. Another method is to list on separate sheets of paper those chores that should be done daily, weekly, and monthly. Number the chores listed on each sheet. Place in three bowls pieces of paper that have numbers written on them that correspond to the chores listed on the sheets of paper. Decide how many pieces of paper each person should draw from each of the three bowls. You may want younger children to draw fewer chores. Let each person take a turn at drawing one piece of paper from each bowl. As the pieces of paper are drawn, write the chore corresponding to the number drawn onto a chore chart. The chart should list the chores that are to be performed by person and by day. Leave space on the chart for the person to mark when the chore is completed. In order to be fair, you may want to draw new assignments each week, or you may want to simply rotate assignments after a certain period of time.
*			*	Encourage all members of the family to be responsible for keeping the home clean by playing "Doozie Nowzie" (do it now). The Doozie Nowzie monster is a pillowcase decorated to look like a hungry monster. (Some parents have called the bag the "Grunge Bag" or the "Gunny Monster.") When the monster growls loud enough for the children to hear, he goes into a room and looks for things left lying on the floor that he can "eat" by picking them up and placing them into a bag. Give the children a few moments before going into a room so that they can rapidly clean up. If the Doozie Nowzie monster "eats" something, the child will have to do a special chore to get it back or wait for a period of time until it is earned back.

Support (*continued*)

Best Practice	High Travel Solution	Spouse Focused	Children Focused	Action Item
*			*	Prepare meals together as a family. Assign one day a week for a child to help Mom or Dad in creating a meal. Allow some creativity, perhaps allowing the children to use their own unique spices or flavorings for the various foods.
		*	*	Create a tradition of "Everybody Help Time" after the meal, when all family members work to quickly clean up the kitchen. It is also a time to talk and ask questions about school, work, hobbies, and sports.

Equal Partnership and Respect				
Best Practice	**High Travel Solution**	**Spouse Focused**	**Children Focused**	**Action Item**
*		*		Allow your spouse personal "getaway" time, such as time alone to read, study, shop, or just be free of family and home duties.
		*		Share or periodically switch child-care roles. If you work during the week, offer to do all the home chores on Saturday and Sunday.
		*	*	Cook meals together. Try experimenting with cooking new meals together.
			*	Encourage meaningful work responsibilities for children at home. These work assignments may be in the form of household chores or of taking care of other siblings. Share in the chore responsibility along with the children.
		*	*	Show visible affection for your spouse in front of the children. Show appropriate physical displays of affection.
		*	*	Express appreciation, respect, and reverence for your spouse in front of the children as well as in private. Compliment him or her on the work he or she has done in the home or the time he or she has spent with the children.

Equal Partnership and Respect (*continued*)

Best Practice	High Travel Solution	Spouse Focused	Children Focused	Action Item
		*		Express appreciation publicly for the work your spouse does away from the home. Openly compliment your spouse on her or his work outside of the home.
		*		Assess fairness in the home. Evaluate whether responsibilities and privileges are distributed fairly among family members. Take into consideration age, maturity, and abilities when looking at fairness. Ask your spouse and your children if they think there is a fair distribution.
		*	*	Recognize and praise those who help others with their chores, homework, or other responsibilities.
			*	Institute an award for "family teamwork" and recognize an individual's achievement with a ribbon, a plaque, or a small memento.
		*		Play role reversal with your spouse for a day. Reverse the roles in the house by swapping who cooks, cleans, takes care of the children, bathes the baby, and so on.
			*	Teach children to take initiative and responsibility for chores around the house (e.g., if clothes are dirty, wash them rather than waiting for Mom or Dad to do them; if the kitchen is dirty, clean it up; and so on).
			*	Teach children that possessions are "ours" and that they have responsibility for caring for our house, our car, our neighborhood, and so on.
		*		Establish a set time each week for each spouse to take a turn cooking, even if one spouse cooks only once during the week. Establish a set time for a child to help cook.
*			*	Divide the home up into areas and assign each area to a specific person, who is to be responsible for it, monitor it, and clean it up on a daily or weekly basis. Rather than assign chores, assign an area and all chores for the area (vacuuming, dusting, picking up, and so on).

Creation of an Action Plan

After you have identified the top five behaviors that you do well, use the family council to identify one or two actions that you can take to leverage your strengths and apply them in different ways. For example, if one of your behavioral strengths is "taking time to have personal conversations," you can plan additional ways to have good one-on-one communication, such as through planned dates with your spouse or the children or by scheduling a specific time to call home each day. In addition, identify the five behaviors that need the most attention. Use the family council to identify one or two actions that will help you improve in the areas that need attention. For example, if you have difficulty being "patient with all family members," you may want to identify from the Best Practices Guide some ways to cool down or keep your impatience in check. For example, you may want to charge yourself $10 and place it in a jar for a fun family activity every time you are impatient.

Write each action in the action plan form given here, including details of when you will begin the action and how you will know whether the action is helping you develop the behavior you want. You may want to schedule another family council to discuss your progress with the family and whether the action was helpful.

Action Plan: What I Will Do	When/How Often I Will Implement the Action	How I Will Know the Action Is Effective
1.		

Action Plan Form (*continued*)

Action Plan: What I Will Do	When/How Often I Will Implement the Action	How I Will Know the Action Is Effective
2.		
3.		

CHAPTER 9

Relationship Behaviors

"Your family and your love must be cultivated like a garden. Time, effort, and imagination must be summoned constantly to keep any relationship flourishing and growing."

—Jim Rohn

RELATIONSHIP BEHAVIORS ARE those behaviors that help a relationship develop and grow. They include demonstrating love, spending time, keeping commitments, and having fun. Relationship behaviors build upon and strengthen the core behaviors. They require a greater investment of time and energy and commitment of the heart, yet they yield a greater return on personal investment.

Larry was the proud owner of a new luxury automobile. He had made it very clear to the members of his family that they would not be allowed to bring food into or eat in his new car. One day his 9-year-old son, Scott, needed a ride to a sports activity. His father agreed to take him and pulled the car out of the garage. In his haste to make it on time, Scott hopped into the car while still eating his lunch. Before his father could say a word, he accidentally smeared some of his peanut butter sandwich on the leather of the door. The father went ballistic with his son, yelling at him for his careless act. Scott was a quiet type who said little and displayed little emotion. On this occasion, he quietly looked down into his lap as his father yelled at him. When Larry had finished,

Scott looked up with tears in his eyes and said, "You love this car more than me, don't you?" Larry was stunned. He was ashamed that he was putting material things ahead of his relationship with his son. What was more disheartening was that his son realized where he stood relative to the other things that were important in Larry's life.

Individuals who exhibit relationship behaviors put a priority on the relationship—a relationship that will endure long after a car or a house or a disagreement is gone. Their commitment to their personal and family relationships results in more dedication of time and effort to nurturing and growing these relationships, a higher quality and a greater quantity of time. And they know how to have fun with their family. For example, the president of a consumer business was a hard worker and spent hours at work, but he always attended all his son's football games. Usually that meant that he took half a day off on Friday to drive there. But it was on his calendar, and he worked around it. He made himself available to his colleagues at work at all other times.

Another senior executive kept the promise she had made to her son to attend an event that was important to him, even though it meant cutting short a meeting with the state attorney general. This sent a powerful message throughout her office that family and personal priorities were on an equal footing with work priorities and that employees should never feel guilty for dealing with conflicts to the advantage of their personal and family relationships.

Sometimes the commitment to personal and family relationships requires the sacrifice of some personal time, social time, and hobbies. As a senior executive put it:

> What do you get rid of to get the quantity of time you need with the family? TV, spectator sports, pure socializing? It's a sacrifice. Over the years I've gotten to the point where I say to people at work, "I will go to your wedding and your wake, but that's it—I can't go socialize all the time."

Family 360 Survey Tool for Relationship Behaviors: Demonstrating Love, Dedicating Time to the Relationship, and Bringing Integrity and Fun to the Relationship

(For a full explanation of the steps in conducting the survey, see Chapter 7.) Prior to giving the Family 360 survey to your family, take a few minutes and evaluate yourself. How are you doing on these relationship behaviors? Look through the following list of 23 questions and score yourself on how well you exhibit the relationship behaviors. Use your self-scored highs to identify your strengths and your lows to identify areas for improvement and look through the Best Practices Guide for ideas on how to leverage your strengths and improve on areas that need attention. Then give the Family 360 survey to your family and compare your self-assessment scores with those of your family members.

FAMILY 360 SURVEY: *Relationship Behavior Questions*

Demonstrating Love							
	Needs Significant Attention	Needs Some Attention	Almost Acceptable	Acceptable	More than Acceptable	Strength	Significant Strength
18. Says "I love you" often enough	O	O	O	O	O	O	O
19. Shows love by the things he or she does	O	O	O	O	O	O	O
20. Creates an environment of love when together	O	O	O	O	O	O	O

Relationship Behavior Questions/Demonstrating Love (*continued*)

	Needs Significant Attention	Needs Some Attention	Almost Acceptable	Acceptable	More than Acceptable	Strength	Significant Strength
21. Uses a kind voice when speaking	O	O	O	O	O	O	O
22. Makes others feel important	O	O	O	O	O	O	O
23. Is a true friend	O	O	O	O	O	O	O
24. Kindly respects differences of opinion	O	O	O	O	O	O	O
25. Talks with children about their important events and activities (i.e., school work, etc.)	O	O	O	O	O	O	O
Integrity							
26. Keeps promises	O	O	O	O	O	O	O
27. Apologizes when he or she has done something wrong or has hurt others' feelings	O	O	O	O	O	O	O
28. Encourages everyone to participate in making family decisions	O	O	O	O	O	O	O

Relationship Behavior Questions/Integrity (*continued*)

	Needs Significant Attention	Needs Some Attention	Almost Acceptable	Acceptable	More than Acceptable	Strength	Significant Strength
29. Keeps a secret when asked	O	O	O	O	O	O	O
Dedication of Time							
30. Spends unhurried time with family members	O	O	O	O	O	O	O
31. Does fun things with family members	O	O	O	O	O	O	O
32. Spends regular one-on-one time with family members (e.g., dates, heart-to-heart talks, etc.)	O	O	O	O	O	O	O
33. Is flexible in his or her schedule to spend time with family members	O	O	O	O	O	O	O
34. Spends time with the children doing things they enjoy	O	O	O	O	O	O	O
35. Spends time with the children when they need help	O	O	O	O	O	O	O

Relationship Behavior Questions/Dedication of Time (*continued*)

	Needs Significant Attention	Needs Some Attention	Almost Acceptable	Acceptable	More than Acceptable	Strength	Significant Strength
36. Participates in the children's important events and activities	O	O	O	O	O	O	O
37. Encourages weekly "date night" with spouse	O	O	O	O	O	O	O
Fun and Humor							
38. Has a way of making things more fun and enjoyable	O	O	O	O	O	O	O
39. Initiates fun recreational activities	O	O	O	O	O	O	O
40. Has a sense of humor that is appreciated	O	O	O	O	O	O	O

Big Idea 2: One-on-One Dates with Spouse and Children

By far the most common action that busy people have implemented to improve their relationships is regularly scheduled one-on-one "dates." These events take on the same feeling of romance and fun that they had during a couple's initial courtship. From our survey work, more than 20 percent of our survey respondents cited a regularly scheduled date with their spouse as the most important and helpful action they took to strengthen their relationship. Generally, the respondents tried to have a date at least once every 2 weeks.

Because of conflicting schedules, one-on-one dates with a spouse tend to be planned. Some people put a specific event on the calendar weeks ahead of time; others scheduled a specific time on the calendar and then did something spontaneous.

- "We have a standing 'night out' every other Saturday, with a babysitter already scheduled, so that my wife and I can spend time alone together."
- "The biggest single activity we have had is a 'routine date night.' It helps us have good conversation and continually maintain our focus on our priorities."
- "I work a stagger shift, with a 12-hour day. I make a point of having a 'date night' with my wife on my shift break nights off. We go out to dinner and maybe the movies, or even shop together."
- "My wife wants more adult conversation. She is home alone all day with the kids. So about every 2 weeks we go on a date, just like when we were dating. It makes a tremendous difference in our communication."
- "We have a standing date for every Friday. We started it when the kids were small, and we still do it now that all of the children are out of the house. Sometimes it is just a trip to the ice cream shop or a trip to the mall to go shopping. But we always manage to get out and away."

Dates with a spouse often took place on the spur of the moment. Some of the most memorable dates were spontaneous gestures of thoughtfulness.

- "Some of my favorite dates have been going to local plays in the park—not just going to the movies. We would just decide to go."
- "After a Sunday afternoon nap, I came downstairs to find that my husband had made a beautiful, romantic meal, with lighted candles, flowers, and music on the stereo. It was a wonderful date, and we didn't even need to go anywhere."
- "We decided on the spur of the moment to fly to Europe. We didn't have any reservations—we just went. That was my most memorable date."

One-on-one dates take on added meaning when they celebrate an important occasion, such as a birthday or an anniversary. But they can also take on added meaning and create strong memories when they celebrate a less important occasion or a "nonoccasion," such as the anniversary of the first date, anniversary of the first year in a new location, anniversary of graduation from college, and so on.

Dates can also be regularly scheduled with children: mother/daughter dates, father/daughter dates, mother/son dates, or father/son dates.

- "The one-on-one time with my children is very special and very critical. I have found through my one-on-ones with them that what's going on internally is not always what's showing on the outside."
- "My husband and I take turns giving each of our three children a special day in which my husband or I spend one-on-one time together with one child. These days are very popular with the children. The child can choose the activity (sledding, a museum, a show) of his or her liking, and we usually have a snack or a meal out."
- "We have routine 'date nights' with our five children individually. It really helps us to remain open in our communications."

These one-on-one dates do not have to be spectacular or elaborate. Frequently we find that the best way to create lasting memories with family members is not through big vacations to exotic places, but through simply being with family members, taking time with them, talking with them, showing them that you care by being with them.

I decided to take a day off from work and spend some time with my 9-year-old son. We decided to take a hike in the mountains of Colorado, where we lived. I had been heavily involved with work for several weeks straight, and I thought that a 1-day break would be good for both me and my son. We drove to a hiking trail and left our car. As we began our journey up the trail, we met the caretaker of the property through which we were passing. He told us that it was springtime and that we needed to be careful not to get caught in between a mother bear and her cubs. He told us to make lots of noise so that the bears would be scared away. He also let us borrow his magnum .455 just for some added protection. As we made our way up the mountain trail, we looked for bears, made lots of noise, and explored old abandoned mining camps and homesteads. At the top of the trail we carefully shot at targets against a bank of earth with the handgun. My son had an opportunity to hold the gun with me, look down the sights, and feel the kick of the gun. He loved to see the dirt kick up when it hit our targets placed against the dirt bank. It was an experience he had never had before. Eventually, the sun started to go down and it was time to head on down the trail, return the gun, and drive home. Just about the time we got to the car, my son turned to me and said, "Dad, this is the best day of my whole life, thanks." I thought of all the trips we had taken to the beach or to amusement parks, and yet all it took to create a lasting memory was a little time off for some one-on-one and a little creativity.

One-on-one dates with children are a perfect way to get to know them without their feeling that you are interrogating them or peppering them with all sorts of probing questions. Information from children comes out most easily when they are having fun, doing something enjoyable, and getting some attention from Mom or Dad.

- "My children enjoy the one-on-one time with me. We usually do something fun, and in the process of doing something fun, we just talk. I find out all sorts of things I never knew—what's happening at school, who they like, where they are having difficulty in school. I don't think I could find this out any other way than mixing some fun with talking."

- "I used to spend a lot of time one-on-one with my children, trying to ask questions, interviewing them, and trying to make sure that we had a good connection. I found I was developing a bad habit of communicating by inquisition. They started seeing me as the host of a quiz game show. It made me feel more like an interrogator than a concerned father. So I decided to spend the time either playing games with them or doing something fun instead. We did one-on-one dates, either staying at home to play games or going out on the town. And we were able to discuss some of the same things, but while we were doing something fun."

163

One-on-one dates can be particularly helpful for single parents, allowing them to stay connected with their children. Frequently, the single parent has significant pressures to provide for the family, spend time at work, maintain the house, care for the children, and take care of his or her own social life. Time does not come easily for the single parent, but time on a date with a child is time well spent.

- "As a single parent, I see this one-on-one time with my child as the most important thing I can do. I work hard while he is at school and day care so that we can have some good time together."
- "I have been divorced for 15 years and have had no time to build another relationship. I tried to develop a good relationship with my son, particularly for the years when he was in high school and prior to his going to college. We always set aside time to do something together. In order to spend as much time with him as possible, I learned to sail and ski because that is what he wanted to do."

Big Idea 3: Family Night

Another variation of Big Idea 1 (family council) is the family night. As mentioned in Chapter 8, a family council is an administrative tool which helps a family run smoothly, cooperatively, and as a close unit. It is a tool to jointly establish family rules and expectations for behavior and to coordinate family schedules and activities. A family night is the cousin of the family council and focuses more on building and improving the relationships within the family— learning together and having fun together.

The Purpose of Family Night

The purpose of the family night is to spend time together, whether as a couple (if you do not have children) or as an entire family. The focus of the night is having fun together. A secondary focus can be serving together or learning something new together. But the focus is on fun and building memories of laughter and friendship that can last a lifetime.

Key Components of Family Night

Do an activity together as a family. It can be something as simple as baking a cake together, playing games, going for a hike, gazing at the stars, roasting marshmallows over the grill, telling jokes, or having a candlelight dinner in the kitchen. The only limit is your imagination and the time needed to plan and prepare.

Talk, ask questions, listen. Many of the activities will produce their own discussion and talk.

Look for opportunities to teach principles. Don't force it, but as you plan and prepare the activities to do as a family, plan for the kinds of topics you can discuss.

- If you bake a cake, think about how you can bring in a discussion of working as a team or of how every ingredient (and member of the family) is important.
- If you play games, think how you can talk about fairness, honesty, being a good sport, compassion (letting your younger brother win), or thinking strategically.
- If you travel to visit a museum, think about how you can talk about developing skills and talents.

Have a treat together. Members of the family can take turns preparing the treat, such as marshmallow squares, ice cream sundaes, or favorite traditional desserts. Sometimes the actual family night activity can consist of making the dessert together as a family.

How to Hold a Family Night

Step 1. ***Establish one night of the week to hold the family night and plan for your activity.*** Use the Best Practices Guide to select activities, or ask the members of your family what they would like to do. Always holding family night on one specific evening of the week can help get people to set the time aside—everyone knows ahead of time when it will be, so they can plan to leave it open. (For example, one town in northern New Jersey set aside Monday night as its community-wide family night and asked teachers not to give too much homework that evening and sports leagues not to schedule games on that night so that the families in the community could have time together as a family. The evening was well received, since the majority of parents had been feeling the pain of being overscheduled as families.)

Step 2. *Involve family members in planning and carrying out the activity.* If you play games as a family, ask someone to select two games to play that night. If you are going out to eat as a family, rotate the selection of the location through each member of the family. If you are going to make dinner or a dessert together, ask family members to help plan and fix the food. The length of the activity does not matter—it can be as short as 15 minutes or as long as several hours. The important goal of the activity is to have fun together and talk together.

Step 3. *Eat the treat together.* These desserts should be some of the family's favorites. A good treat after having a fun time is a great way to end the activity. Furthermore, a treat at the end of the activity goes a long way toward encouraging family members to participate.

Critical Success Factors for Family Night

1. *Focus on having fun.* Families can have fun together whether they are playing games in the family room or serving together at a soup kitchen. Try to keep the occasion upbeat and positive, and avoid any personal criticism, even if a family member does something you do not like. You want to coax every family member to come back the next time, and the only way to do that is to keep family night fun and light.

   - "We have so much fun when we do game night as a family. We just don't do it often enough."
   - "Sometimes we will just read stories that are fun to read or that teach a moral. Sometimes we will play games. But we will always have something good to eat at the end. We can devour an entire tray of homemade brownies and a half-gallon of milk in just a few minutes."

- "We have gotten into the habit, so everyone knows that the evening is for the family. Making it fun and involving the children is key."

2. *Involve all family members in selecting the activity.* Until you have some experience under your belt and all family members feel that the family night is worthwhile, you will need to get their personal involvement by involving them in the selection and planning of the evening's activity.

3. *Select a dessert that everyone will enjoy.* The family that eats together, stays together. Don't underestimate the power of a good dessert to keep family members interested in the entire activity.

Solutions from the Best Practices Guide

The following actions come from the many people we have worked with over the years and the descriptions they have given of ways in which they built and strengthened their personal relationships. In essence, these actions have been tested in real life and may prove helpful for you. (See Chapter 7 for a full description of how to make the most effective use of the Best Practices Guide.)

Demonstrating Love				
Best Practice	**High Travel Solution**	**Spouse Focused**	**Children Focused**	**Action Item**
*	*	*	*	Leave surprise Post-it note messages for family members. Leave unexpected notes of appreciation or love in locations where family members will find them during the day, or in the evening if you will be away at night—in a lunch box, on the bathroom mirror, on the pillow, in their shoe, and so on.
	*	*	*	Carry envelopes and blank cards in your briefcase or notebook, where they are easily accessible to you. Write letters of love and appreciation to your family members, regardless of where you travel. Send them while you are away from home, or pre-send them so that they will arrive while you are away.

Demonstrating Love (*continued*)

Best Practice	High Travel Solution	Spouse Focused	Children Focused	Action Item
		*		Start a "just cus" habit: Buy flowers, go out to dinner, send a special note, go out on the town, go to the movies, and so on, "just cus you love each other." A special occasion (e.g., a birthday or an anniversary) is not needed to do small, thoughtful acts of love.
		*		Call home. Make phone calls home during breaks or during lunch just to say hi and to see how things are going. Call sometimes for no reason at all.
*		*	*	During a special occasion (e.g., Thanksgiving, a birthday celebration, or New Year's), have family members write on 3" x 5" cards what they appreciate most about each other family member. Read the thoughts out loud to the entire family or give the cards to the family members to read privately.
			*	Institute a "daily dose of love." This activity can be done with the entire family or by you with particular family members. Discuss with your spouse and/or your children specific actions that they believe help them to feel loved. For example, ask them to complete the phrase "I feel most loved when someone . . ." The actions stated should be simple and clearly defined. Have each person write down the actions on the part of each other person that help her or him feel loved on a separate list. Have each person pick two or three actions that he or she would like to see demonstrated toward him or her on a daily basis. Discuss the selections. For 2 weeks, each person in the family should make a special effort to perform each action daily. After 2 weeks, talk about how those actions made each person feel loved and appreciated. Discuss the difference it made in the family. Select additional actions from your list to try out during the next 2 weeks.
		*	*	Eliminate relationship procrastination for 1 week. Throughout any given day, ideas on ways to improve your relationships may come to you. Some of these ideas may be real inspirations. You

Demonstrating Love (*continued*)

Best Practice	High Travel Solution	Spouse Focused	Children Focused	Action Item
				can choose to write these ideas down in your day planner or Palm Pilot so that you remember to do them later. However, for 1 week, if you feel prompted to do some action to improve or strengthen your relationships, act on it immediately, if at all possible. For example, if you feel you need to apologize to your husband for being impatient with him, stop what you are doing at work and call him to say so. If your child went into her room after an argument and you feel the need to apologize, do so immediately. Act on your intuition immediately throughout the week.
		*		Identify two or three things that you appreciate most about your spouse or your children (e.g., helpfulness around the house, helping with the dishes, doing homework promptly, or getting up and going to school on time). Write these things on a card and put it in your pocket as a reminder. Throughout the week, express your appreciation to this person for these things. Look for additional things that this person does that you appreciate and write them on the card also.
		*	*	Surprise your spouse or your family by making a candlelight dinner for no special reason. Turn off all the lights in the house except for the candles.
		*	*	Block out time and make an "incremental investment." As you consider your relationship with your spouse or your child, think of one thing that you could do if you had an additional hour each week to spend in strengthening or building your relationship with that person. You might consider going for a walk, sitting together and having an uninterrupted conversation, or playing a game. Think in terms of what activity would mean most to the other person. For 1 month, commit to investing that additional hour each week. Track your progress and activities on a piece of paper. At the end of the month, evaluate whether the time has been invested wisely. If so, continue the activity. If not, change it to something that is more valuable.

Demonstrating Love (*continued*)

Best Practice	High Travel Solution	Spouse Focused	Children Focused	Action Item
		*		Renew your marriage vows. Return to the place where you were married and review the marital commitments you made to each other. Invite a few family members or friends to witness the occasion, and afterward hold an informal reception.
		*		Share your appreciation for your spouse. Together with him or her, list the ways in which your lives have been enriched during the time you have been together.
		*	*	Write a letter of gratitude to your spouse for the ways in which he or she has blessed your life and leave it on his or her pillow. Any day or occasion is a good occasion for this. This process can be used to express appreciation for a child as well.
		*	*	Squeeze in little surprises. Give a little flower, a cookie, or a special treat for no reason at all. Bring home the chocolate mint they put on the hotel pillow or the candy they served on the plane. Hide the surprises to add an element of fun and spontaneity.
			*	Begin to have periodic visits at night from the "Shoe Fairy"—a cherubic little imp who leaves special notes or treats in the shoes of all family members during the night.
		*	*	Give physical expressions of love, in whatever form. Show you care with a little pat, a hug, a kiss, a handclasp, or an arm around the shoulder. Don't be shy about showing appropriate physical expressions of love toward your spouse around the children, or about physical expressions of love toward your children.
		*	*	Give a gift certificate of time. Write or print a certificate that gives a specific family member the gift of your time—for example, "Certificate: Good for One Hour of Time to Go to the Ice Cream Store" or "Good for One Hour of Doing Whatever You Want to Do."

Demonstrating Love (*continued*)

Best Practice	High Travel Solution	Spouse Focused	Children Focused	Action Item
		*		Read old love letters or notes that you and your spouse wrote to each other during your courting or early years. Put them in a book similar to a photo album.
		*	*	Discuss moments of success. During a family council, ask, "When was one moment when our family was very close?" "When did our family really pull together and support one another?" "When do we love one another the most?" Based on the responses, plan an activity to replicate what was identified.
*			*	Designate "secret pals." A week prior to a special day, such as Valentine's Day or Christmas, have each family member draw a name from a hat and then, throughout the week, do secret, nice deeds or services for the person whose name was drawn. At the end of the week, disclose the identity of each of the secret pals.
			*	Create a family sign or signal that means "I love you." Use the sign when you are in a crowded room or in public. For example, the sign could be a hand signal from a distance, a funny face, or three squeezes of the hand.
	*	*	*	If you will be gone for an extended period of time, send a brief letter ahead of time, to arrive shortly after you depart. Express your feelings of love and compliment the person for the attributes you most appreciate.
	*		*	Send a love note to a child, addressed to her or him at school c/o the class teacher.
*				Prepare for your reentry into your home. Use your commuting time to ratchet down your pace. Listen to classical or relaxing music rather than the news or the latest stock report. Before you arrive, try to match your pace and intensity to the environment of your home. Recognize that your spouse or your children may be functioning on a different frequency from yours.

Demonstrating Love (*continued*)

Best Practice	High Travel Solution	Spouse Focused	Children Focused	Action Item
				Take the long route home instead of the short. Create a long and a short route from work. On those days when you're feeling especially stressed and impatient, take the long route home to give yourself a few extra minutes to change gears for home.
			*	Talk about people's feelings with your children —how others feel if we hurt them, are dishonest with them, ignore them, and so on. Use specific problems or experiences in the family as a focus for talking about feelings and how a sibling, parent, or friend may feel.
		*	*	Conduct a start, stop, and keep doing exercise with your spouse and your children. Tell them that you want them to be your "personal coach" to help you learn how to be better at demonstrating love. Provide them with a piece of paper and ask them to write the answers to three questions. Allow approximately 3 to 5 minutes to write answers to the following questions: • "What would you like me to start doing differently in order to demonstrate my love for you?" • "What would you like me to stop doing in order to demonstrate my love for you?" • "What would you like me to keep doing in order to demonstrate my love for you?" Then have each person present her or his answers. You should be prepared just to listen and to agree on one or two things that you are going to start, stop, and keep doing.
*		*	*	Periodically have a family night meeting where the only activity is taking turns expressing love and appreciation for one another. Take turns saying what you admire most in each family member and the qualities and characteristics that you appreciate the most. Write the comments down and give the summary to each family member to reread over the next few weeks.

Integrity				
Best Practice	**High Travel Solution**	**Spouse Focused**	**Children Focused**	**Action Item**
*				Encourage high values and service through your own behavior. Talk with your family about your highest values and what you do to stay committed to them. Openly discuss times when you did not live your personal values and how you felt about this.
*			*	Create a set of family values—what is most important, and how the family can help everyone live by those values. Write the agreed-upon values on a chart and display them in a prominent location in the home. Revisit them every few months to see how the family is doing in relation to the values. (*Note:* Parents should be careful not to establish a double standard, with one set of values for the adults and another for the children—adults should be expected to live by the same values as children.)
		*	*	When you make a mistake, admit it openly to the family. Let other family members know that it is okay for them to make mistakes as well.
			*	Use a good planning system and calendar. Incorporate all promises and family council commitments into a Personal Digital Assistant (PDA), scheduler, or planner for future follow-through and review.
*			*	Play "What would you do?" with real-life examples *from your own life.* Discuss with family members specific situations that you encounter at work or outside the home where your values and standards are put to the test—for example, being asked to share confidential information with a friend, being given credit for work that you did not do, or observing a coworker taking something that did not belong to him or her. Without naming specific people, share enough details of the circumstances to allow your family to understand your experience. Talk about the issues involved. Ask for their ideas about or

Integrity (*continued*)

Best Practice	High Travel Solution	Spouse Focused	Children Focused	Action Item
				solutions to the situation. Talk about your resolution of the situation. Discuss how values that are important to you influenced your decision. Ask others to share similar experiences.
*			*	Play "What would you do?" *with possible dilemmas that could be faced by your children.* Ask them how they would handle these dilemmas. For example, you are late in reading a book and preparing your book report. Your friend offers to tell you what happens in the book and share his ideas for the book report. What would you do? (*Note:* There is a card game called "Kid's Choices," published by Rainfall, that gives a wide range of ethical, moral, and decision dilemmas to discuss with your children.)

Dedication of Time

Best Practice	High Travel Solution	Spouse Focused	Children Focused	Action Item
*				Carefully prioritize your activities at work and at home. Involve family members in an open discussion of work and personal priorities. Work together as a family to establish priorities and manage to those priorities. Use a family calendar to schedule and plan events.
*		*		Hold a regular one-on-one date with your spouse. These dates should be scheduled along with other high-priority activities. Plan the type of event or date jointly with your spouse and place it on your business and personal calendars.
*			*	Hold a regular one-on-one date with each of your children. These dates should be scheduled along with other high-priority activities. Plan the type of event jointly with the child, and place it on your business and personal calendars.
*		*	*	Put all activities on your calendar. Effectively blend your work and personal calendars to give proper attention to all activities.

Dedication of Time (*continued*)

Best Practice	High Travel Solution	Spouse Focused	Children Focused	**Action Item**
*			*	Schedule regular father/daughter, father/son, mother/daughter, or mother/son interviews. Set aside 20 minutes at least once each month to talk one-on-one with each of your children and ask them questions about how they are doing—how they are doing in school, who their best friends are and why, what they want to become when they grow up, what their talents are, what talents they would like to develop, what their favorite food is, and so on.
*	*			Utilize resources more effectively. If possible, pay others to do such activities as house chores, yard work, and car repairs in order to save time for other higher-priority activities with the family.
*	*			Institute a planning calendar at work that allows all department members to place their important and critical family activities on the work calendar in order to minimize disruption to their most important family activities.
*	*			Place all your important personal appointments on your work calendar, including birthdays, anniversaries, important sports events, and so on.
*	*			Block out family time on weekends. Priorities are best maintained when they are scheduled on the calendar and protected from other activities that might interfere, particularly during the weekend.
		*	*	Purchase a calendar or day planner for each member of the family and teach them how to use it. Coordinate your individual calendars at least once per week.
*		*		Loosen your standards for housekeeping. Deliberately reduce the requirements or standards for housekeeping so that more time is available for relationship-building activities.
		*	*	Create a "no housekeeping" zone or time in which major cleaning is not done, such as during a vacation or during a specific weekend or holiday.

Dedication of Time (*continued*)

Best Practice	High Travel Solution	Spouse Focused	Children Focused	Action Item
*				Reassess your workload and processes at work in order to have more time at home. Evaluate your workload to determine processes that can be streamlined or eliminated. Create a formal objective of eliminating work and streamlining work processes. Evaluate each work component against other components to establish high-value and low-value activities.
*	*	*	*	Discuss work and family goals together as a family. Openly share the challenges and demands placed on you by your work. Share the objectives you have as a family and your work objectives, then strive together as a family to establish and manage work and family priorities.
*		*	*	Eliminate or reduce TV watching in the house for 1 week. Spend the time playing games, helping one another with homework, or doing community service.
				Consider not replacing TVs when they break.
				Use either parental blocks on TVs or timers to limit the amount of time children and adults spend watching TV.
				During family councils, dinnertime, or other such occasions, shut off the phone or allow it to ring to an answering machine.
*		*	*	Schedule time for a weekly date with your spouse and place it on your work *and* personal calendars well ahead of time. Schedule regular time for joint family activities and blend it with existing work and personal demands.
*		*		Participate in fitness activities together as a couple or as a family. Spend time together while pursuing an exercise regimen or some other physical activity, such as hiking, dancing, or biking.
	*	*	*	Make daily contact by phone. Schedule a specific time on your work calendar to make midday phone calls to your spouse and/or to your children.

Dedication of Time (*continued*)

Best Practice	High Travel Solution	Spouse Focused	Children Focused	Action Item
*		*	*	Identify and participate jointly in common hobbies, as a couple or as a family.
*		*	*	Participate in joint service projects or community involvement activities.
*	*	*	*	Involve your spouse and/or your children in business trips, if possible. If finances allow, occasionally take your spouse or your older children with you on a business trip.
			*	Include family members in errands. Take a child with you when you go to the store, get a haircut, stop by the library, or run other errands.
			*	Take advantage of "Take Your Children to Work" Day. Bring your children to work periodically so that they can see where you work and what you do during the day.
	*		*	Maximize your use of commute time or travel time by recording your personal history or stories of your youth on a cassette recorder. Share these stories with your family. Make a tape for children who no longer live at home or a personal tape for a special occasion for a member of your family.
	*		*	Maximize your use of commute time or travel time by recording your thoughts and feelings on a tape for children who no longer live at home or a personal tape for a special occasion (e.g., wedding, graduation, first job, birth of a child, etc.) for a member of your family.
*				As much as possible, make home a work-free zone. Leave work pressures and frustrations at work. Allow your home environment to be free from work frustrations.
*				Eat meals together. Make dinnertime a time for sharing the day's activities and experiences. Keep the conversations light and pleasant.
				Institute a "linger longer" period after dinner. Use the time to clean up together after the meal or just to sit and talk for a few minutes longer.

Dedication of Time (*continued*)

Best Practice	High Travel Solution	Spouse Focused	Children Focused	Action Item
	*	*	*	If you travel frequently, read bedtime stories ahead of time into a cassette recorder or video recorder for your children. Leave a cassette recording for your spouse.
		*	*	Set aside a specific time each day to pay a compliment, encourage a talent, write a note or letter of appreciation, or do other similar activities—for example, the first 10 minutes after you arrive home from work, immediately prior to bedtime, or right after dinner. Setting aside a specific time encourages you to remember to do the activity.
	*		*	Set aside a specific time to help your children with their homework. Help them plan for long-term projects. If you are traveling, call at a preset time to discuss and review their homework.
			*	Read to your children regularly. For example, read a popular book as a family right after dinner. Teach them the beauty of literature. Select books that they will enjoy and eagerly anticipate.
			*	Volunteer to work at your child's school, chaperone a school field trip, read books to the class, help with work assignments, plan a party, or talk about your career.
			*	Offer to teach a class for a group of children on a fun topic on which you have expertise (e.g., crafts, hobbies, or cooking). Volunteer to teach the class at school or volunteer to teach the class for neighborhood children.
			*	Invite the friends of members of your family to a fun family evening. Plan and carry out the evening with your children, with dinner, food, games, a movie, or something else. Draw up a special invitation to invite a friend of a child or several friends to participate.
*		*	*	Arrange to do all your house chores together as a family, going from one room to the next and working together until each room is clean. Set a timer, then try to work fast and beat the buzzer, but talk as you go.

Dedication of Time (*continued*)

Best Practice	High Travel Solution	Spouse Focused	Children Focused	Action Item
			*	Ensure that children have a way to be in contact with you during the day. Establish an agreement that you will stop whatever you are doing at work or at home to discuss something that is important to them.
*				If weekend work is required of you on a regular basis, block out a specific period of time for the work. Reserve the rest of the time for your family and communicate your schedule to them. For example, block out Friday evening to work late and finish your work if that means that the rest of the weekend can be reserved for your family.

Fun and Humor

Best Practice	High Travel Solution	Spouse Focused	Children Focused	Action Item
*			*	Participate in spontaneous activities together. Plan for spontaneity by blocking out a time during the weekend, then deciding what to do or where to go on the spur of the moment.
*	*		*	Plan family adventures. Short trips that are planned in advance can be used as family adventures. Weekend events can be specifically designed to be low-cost and/or short family adventures. Plan adventures while you are traveling so that the family has something to look forward to when you return.
			*	Plan a family adventure by getting in the car and heading out to points unknown. Doing something that has not been done before or that comes as a surprise can make even the most mundane event into an adventure.
*		*	*	Vacation regularly with your spouse and your children. Avoid doing work during vacations.
*		*	*	Plan a regular family game night. Games, movies, home movies, or other fun family activities can be regularly scheduled during the week. Involve all family members in planning the evening.

Fun and Humor (*continued*)

Best Practice	High Travel Solution	Spouse Focused	Children Focused	Action Item
*			*	Identify as a family the important events that you want to attend together, including sports activities, performances, recitals, and so on. Make sure the events are placed on your calendar at work and blocked out as scheduled time.
			*	Earn your dessert. Each family member can earn her or his dessert at dinnertime by telling a funny story or joke. If family members need help, plant a joke under their plate for use in an emergency when they can't think of one.
			*	Create a family song. Select a popular song (for younger children) or a modern piece of pop music (for teenagers) and ask family members to write a new chorus or verse that highlights some activity or family event. Write lyrics that exemplify your family's values.
			*	Create a family joke book. Fill the book with personal anecdotes about the family, funny things members have said, or just jokes that the family thinks are particularly funny.
			*	Create a family scrapbook filled with the funniest pictures and stories—the ones that the children might not want to share with their girl- or boyfriend.
			*	Produce a funny videotape of the family. You could mimic your favorite TV show, play role reversals, or imitate popular TV game shows.
			*	Create your own family sport. Use the family's imagination to develop a game or sport with rules for play and scoring. Consider combining elements of your favorite sports, such as a combination of basketball and tennis for "basketennis." Consider using odd objects found around the house for balls and equipment, such as wooden ladles, rubber bands, Dad's old T-shirt, or a clean diaper, to create crazy and imaginative games.
			*	Create a family Olympics. Measure and track the family "world records" in such areas as the javelin throw (use a straw), the shot put (use a cotton ball), or the high jump.

Fun and Humor (*continued*)

Best Practice	High Travel Solution	Spouse Focused	Children Focused	Action Item
		*	*	Create your own family recipe. Work together to create an original recipe, such as a dinner entrée or a dessert. Decorate the concoction in a humorous way.
	*	*	*	If you travel frequently, give your family members a quiz on the place where you are staying. Fax, email, or phone a "test" of trivia on the location. Use the brochures in the hotel lobby to identify local points of interest for use in your quiz. Frequently there are magazines in the rooms with descriptions of the area's geography, special events, and so on.
	*	*	*	Place humorous notes in strange places to remind the members of your family that you are thinking of them, even when you are away from home. For example, put "I 'a-door' you" on the bathroom door, or "You light up my life" on the lamp in their room, or "If I were there, I would shower you with kisses" in the shower. Use your crazy imagination.
	*		*	Visit your child's school after school has been dismissed for the day and put a special note in his or her desk along with a treat. Or send the note to the teacher and explain that you are traveling and would like the teacher to secretly hide the note in your child's desk.
	*		*	Create unusual and fun adventures, particularly if you are pressed for time or travel frequently. For example, rather than go camping, set up the tent in your living room and camp out with your family. Or set up a card table and chairs in a cozy spot in your home. Light up the barbecue in the middle of winter and grill hamburgers and hot dogs.
		*	*	Light some candles and have your usual dinner by candlelight.
			*	Create a family movie, complete with rough script, plot, amateur acting, music, and commercials. Videotape it in one evening and show it while the family eats popcorn.

181

Fun and Humor (*continued*)

Best Practice	High Travel Solution	Spouse Focused	Children Focused	Action Item
		*	*	Go out for dinner. Consider putting a twist on going out for dinner. For example, go to dinner at 1:00 in the morning at an all-night diner. Or go on a "progressive dinner": appetizers at McDonalds, salad at Wendy's, main course at Burger King, and dessert at a convenience store.
			*	During the wintertime, have a picnic dinner together as a family on the floor of your living room.
			*	Set aside time once a week to cook or bake with each of your children. This is a time to be creative, have fun, and just talk. The food should be something that is chosen by the child.
			*	Work on a craft together. Visit *www.kidsdomain.com/craft* or *www.familyfun.com* for ideas about crafts.
			*	Plan a specific time to have a "spontaneous activity." Planned spontaneity can generate some delightful events. For example, draw activities from a hat, such as go on a midnight hike, play ultimate Frisbee, play hide and seek with flashlights, and so on.
		*	*	Learn a new sport as a family, either a sport that one member does well and can teach to the others or a sport that no one in the family has ever done. For example, consider horseback riding lessons, handball, jet skiing, or mountain biking.
			*	Create a COPE course in your backyard. COPE stands for Challenging Opportunities for Personal Experience. These are exercises and challenges that test individuals' creativity, courage, or physical stamina. They could take the form of an obstacle course, a series of balancing activities, a challenge to retrieve an object from the center of a make-believe circle using only a few provided materials, and so on.
			*	Create a regular family movie night, complete with tickets, reclining seats, and a concession stand with bags of popcorn and candy.

Creation of an Action Plan

After you have identified the top five behaviors that you do well, use the family council to identify one or two actions that you can take to leverage your strengths and apply them in different ways. For example, if one of your behavioral strengths is "making things more fun and enjoyable," you can plan more fun activities using the Best Practices Guide. In addition, identify the five behaviors that need the most attention. Use the family council to identify one or two actions that will help you improve in the areas that need attention. For example, if you have difficulty "spending one-on-one time with family members," you could plan and schedule some small blocks of time for fun activities, or you could schedule a specific time to call home if you are traveling.

Write each action in the action plan form given here, including details of when you will begin the action and how you will know whether the action is helping you develop the behavior you want. You may want to schedule another family council to discuss your progress with the family and whether the action was helpful.

Action Plan: What I Will Do	When/How Often I Will Implement the Action	How I Will Know the Action Is Effective
1.		

Action Plan Form (*continued*)

Action Plan: What I Will Do	When/How Often I Will Implement the Action	How I Will Know the Action Is Effective
2.		
3.		

CHAPTER 10

Growth Behaviors

"Nothing energizes, unites, and satisfies the family like working together to make a significant contribution."

—Stephen R. Covey, *The 7 Habits of Highly Effective Families*

Growth behaviors are driven by our deep personal beliefs and values and to pass on those beliefs and values to our family. They are the efforts we make to teach, build, and encourage the development of personal character, ethics, a sense of worth, and values. They are the behaviors that not only deepen the strength of the individual and the family, but include:

- *Creating a sense of purpose.* Showing the importance of the family unit in society (even if the family unit consists of two people), in helping and serving each other, building traditions, instilling values, and contributing to society.
- *Complimenting, building, and encouraging.* Motivating family members to develop their talents and to achieve a higher level.

- A woman from the United Kingdom described the challenges of raising a family that had gone through divorce and estrangement. Now in her second marriage, with three children from her previous marriage and one from her current marriage, she described what had made a difference in pulling together their family. "It began with one of our first memorable experiences together: when the oldest children were in the room and participated in the birth of my fourth child and the first from my new marriage (at least up until a few minutes prior to the birth). It was a wonderful experience for the family." But after that initial togetherness, the family members grew and developed their own personalities. Some drifted apart, some experienced the difficulties of being independent and headstrong, and some experienced their own divorces and single parenting. What keeps them together? "We have a tradition of being together during the holidays, particularly Christmas, and we have a decades-long tradition of playing games. We love playing games, especially word games like Scrabble and Pass the Bomb (a game that requires you to think and use words quickly) and a good game of darts in the local pub. These games have kept us together, and we always look forward to them."

- A man from the United States who had a large family described the best action he ever took for his family. "The best thing I did for my family happened over 30 years ago. My wife had been working part-time and had saved about $200. She gave it to me as a present and suggested that I buy a suit that I badly needed. I thought about it, and the next day I told her, 'I want to go buy skis for our five children.' So we went down to a used-ski shop in Pennsylvania and bought a set of skis for each person in the family—seven sets of old, used skis for $200. That was the best investment I ever made. Our family tradition of skiing together has created so many memories. Even today, with all the kids in school or married, we get together for skiing, and they always reminisce about all the fun times they had on those old skis."

- "I am divorcing and have one child, so my most important relationship right now is with my daughter. But I also try to keep my daughter in close touch with her many relatives who love her dearly. I think it is important for her to be surrounded by family. With the divorce, I think she needs to know that everyone loves her so much. That is why we are trying to stay connected now more than ever."

- "Setting up the Christmas tree is a big deal at our house. It's a huge event and takes nights and nights to do. I usually don't help because I just don't have the time. This year I actually helped. It was a big thing for the family to have me there for one of our important traditions."

Family 360 Survey Tool for Growth Behaviors: Sense of Purpose; Complimenting, Building, and Encouraging

(For a full explanation of the steps in conducting the survey, see Chapter 7.)

Prior to giving the Family 360 survey to your family, take a few minutes and evaluate yourself. How are you doing on these relationship behaviors? Look through the following list of 15 questions and score yourself on how well you exhibit the relationship behaviors. Use your self-scored highs to identify your strengths and your lows to identify areas for improvement and look through the Best Practices Guide for ideas on how to leverage your strengths and improve on areas that need attention. Then give the Family 360 survey to your family and compare your self-assessment scores with those of your family members.

FAMILY 360 SURVEY: *Growth Behavior Questions*

Sense of Purpose							
	Needs Significant Attention	Needs Some Attention	Almost Acceptable	Acceptable	More than Acceptable	Strength	Significant Strength
41. Helps the family to be united	O	O	O	O	O	O	O
42. Shows by his or her actions that the family is more important than other aspects of life (e.g., work, hobbies, civic responsibilities)	O	O	O	O	O	O	O

Growth Behavior Questions/Sense of Purpose (*continued*)

	Needs Significant Attention	Needs Some Attention	Almost Acceptable	Acceptable	More than Acceptable	Strength	Significant Strength
43. Encourages family members to help and serve others	O	O	O	O	O	O	O
44. Encourages family members to work together	O	O	O	O	O	O	O
45. Helps create enjoyable family traditions (birthdays, holidays, etc.)	O	O	O	O	O	O	O
46. Teaches the children moral values	O	O	O	O	O	O	O
47. Teaches the children responsibility and accountability	O	O	O	O	O	O	O
48. Encourages children to obey the law	O	O	O	O	O	O	O
49. Encourages children to work	O	O	O	O	O	O	O

Growth Behavior Questions (*continued*)

Compliments, Builds, Encourages

	Needs Significant Attention	Needs Some Attention	Almost Acceptable	Acceptable	More than Acceptable	Strength	Significant Strength
50. Shows confidence in family member's abilities to perform well in various aspects of life (e.g., work, school, or sports)	O	O	O	O	O	O	O
51. Compliments family members for their personal achievements	O	O	O	O	O	O	O
52. Gives family members credit for their personal accomplishments	O	O	O	O	O	O	O
53. Helps family members improve their talents	O	O	O	O	O	O	O
54. Encourages family members to keep trying when they are having trouble accomplishing a task	O	O	O	O	O	O	O

Growth Behavior Questions/Compliments, Builds, Encourages (*continued*)

	Needs Significant Attention	Needs Some Attention	Almost Acceptable	Acceptable	More than Acceptable	Strength	Significant Strength
55. Is kind toward family members when they do something wrong	O	O	O	O	O	O	O

Big Idea 4: Giving Family Service

Family service can become a meaningful activity that teaches many important values and instills in the family a sense of purpose and usefulness. In addition, service provides a magical moment when the entire family can feel good about something they are doing. Rarely is there a more powerful feeling of goodwill then when the family serves together.

Family service can be scheduled regularly during the month or can be a spontaneous activity. It can be helpful regardless of family size—whether you are a couple, a family with 10 children, or an extended family with 100 members.

- "We enjoy doing lots of service activities together as a family. Usually we plan and carry out a service activity once a month. We go and visit people at a retirement home, collect donations for needy families, serve in a soup kitchen, or help distribute toys for the holidays, such as with Christmas Unlimited. Our entire family has a wonderful feeling of helping someone as we do these activities."

Service allows the family to experience something that they do not normally see at home. It allows family members to open their hearts to serving and helping others.

- "Service gives our children a sense of purpose, of why they are here in this big world and what they can do to make a bigger impact."
- "It's amazing to see our children see the needs of others, particularly those of other children who may be handicapped or down and out.

They are able to see people who are struggling. For example, we were helping distribute toys to needy people and families at a holiday event. One of my teenage children sat with a participant, who asked 'Are there any coats available?' My children could see that there were many basic needs that were not being met, such as warm clothing. For some families, toys are a luxury. They see a bigger world than just our home."

Service is not limited to immediate family members. Grandmothers and grandfathers, in-laws, and other members of the extended family can provide wonderful opportunities to involve the family in service and to teach values.

- One grandfather, a well-known lecturer, described his effort to help his grandchild give meaningful service. "This grandchild I'm so crazy about called me the day of that shooting at the school. She is 6 years old, and she said 'Oh, papa, can't you do something? All my class is so frightened, and we don't know what to do. We tried to do something before by writing to the congressmen about guns. But,' she added, 'my letter didn't do any good.' I wanted to encourage her and help her feel that she could contribute to society, so I said, 'If you all want to write letters to the President about helping to keep children safe, I will see that he gets them.' So, today this big packet of letters from everyone in her class arrived for me to get to the President."

"Where do I start?" you might ask. You can begin by looking in the Yellow Pages or in the want ads for opportunities to give service. Look up a local retirement or nursing center. Call your local government or community center to find out what is available in the area.

Solutions from the Best Practices Guide

The following actions come from the many people we have worked with over the years and the descriptions they have given of ways in which they built and strengthened their personal relationships. In essence, these actions have been tested in real life and may prove helpful for you. (See Chapter 7 for a full description of how to make the most effective use of the Best Practices Guide.)

Best Practice	High Travel Solution	Spouse Focused	Children Focused	Action Item
				Sense of Purpose
*		*	*	Develop a family legacy vision or mission statement together with all family members. Ask family members to write down what they hope your family will be like 10 to 15 years from now. Read and discuss the comments and what can be done now to help achieve the future vision of the family. Agree to engage in actions or behaviors that will move the family in the direction of the shared vision.
*		*	*	Make service a part of your family time together. Plan a holiday program with parts, music, and treats to be presented at a nursing home. Help at a soup kitchen, prepare bag lunches for the homeless, visit a facility for physically challenged children, help at a homeless shelter, tutor the disabled, donate toys to the needy, deliver food to shut-ins, or take clothes to a recycling center. Visit a retirement home or hospital with family members and just talk with residents or present a program that displays the family's talents.
			*	Attend church or synagogue together as a family.
			*	Encourage responsibility by allowing children to have animals, a garden, or other responsibilities that require work, discipline, and time.
			*	Encourage family members to keep a journal to articulate and record meaningful events or thoughts. Younger children may need help in recording meaningful events or thoughts of the day. Share some of your best thoughts on a designated day each week.
		*	*	Have a regular family time for discussion of spiritual feelings or values. Share your inner spiritual feelings and beliefs.
			*	Assign children household chores. Assign each child tasks at which she or he can be successful. Teach children the necessity and the satisfaction of contributing. Where possible, assign tasks that have two or more family members working together to accomplish the task.

Sense of Purpose (*continued*)

Best Practice	High Travel Solution	Spouse Focused	Children Focused	Action Item
*			*	Create family get-togethers with extended family. Use reunions, birthdays, and holiday celebrations to connect with extended family.
			*	Create opportunities for children to spend time with their grandparents. Activities may include running errands, community service, playing board games, doing puzzles, hunting and fishing, shopping, taking walks, attending church or socials, sharing personal histories, or making phone calls. If the children's grandparents do not live near the home, "adopt" a grandparent from the nearest retirement home or assisted-living facility.
		*	*	Make a "top priority" list. As a family, list 50 of the things you want to do together over the next 25 years. Select one or two of the items to do each year. Schedule those items in your family plan.
	*			Plan family activities ahead of time. Get a 5-year calendar and block out 1 or 2 weeks each year for family vacations. Planning ahead of time is particularly useful when you travel frequently.
			*	Sing together whenever possible, such as when walking, in the car, and especially in the home. Learn how to sing parts and harmonize together.
			*	Teach the other members of your family the songs of your generation. Learn your children's favorite songs. Explore different styles of music, such as rock, country, and classical.
				Take a hike in a pristine area and remove litter.
*				Discover your heritage. Learn about your ancestors, the country they came from, where they lived, what their lifestyle was like, and what they did for a living. Find and review videos, books, magazines, and pictures that relate to the countries your ancestors lived in.
		*	*	Build the family's spiritual strength. Together with your family, make a list of things you want to do to build spiritual strength. The list could

Sense of Purpose (*continued*)

Best Practice	High Travel Solution	Spouse Focused	Children Focused	Action Item
				include participation in religious services, regular family scripture study or other uplifting reading, caring for those in need, or giving service to the community.
		*	*	Plan a specific time each day (perhaps 5 minutes after dinner) or once a week (perhaps 10 minutes on a Sunday evening) to have a family devotional period to read scriptures, discuss spiritual topics, and so on.
			*	Keep the family connected to your extended family. Gather the family around a speaker-phone and call relatives whom you have not spoken to for a while.
			*	Spend a Sunday writing to family members with whom you have not communicated in some time.
			*	Use your extended family to help teach values. Set up a family reunion and ask family members to tell stories about their life and the lives of their ancestors.
				Compile a family history. Provide 3" x 5" cards to each family member and ask them to write down significant family events that they can remember. Collect and read the cards and begin to compile a family history that includes the fun and significant events.
			*	Schedule a "service week." Plan activities for the week that allow family members to serve each other in the family or groups in need outside the family.
				Create, as a family, a family pedigree chart that traces your family heritage. Research genealogy on the Internet and trace your family lines as far back as possible.
*			*	Create bedtime rituals. Routines at bedtime often include storytelling, reminiscing about when the children were younger, recounting funny antics, reading, back rubs, or other quiet activities.

Sense of Purpose (*continued*)

Best Practice	High Travel Solution	Spouse Focused	Children Focused	Action Item
*			*	Develop traditional games and family activities. Some favorite joint activities could include basketball, tennis, camping, mountain biking, Frisbee throwing, baseball, bird watching, and walking. Do these activities during fun times of the year. For example, play football on the morning of Thanksgiving Day, go cross-country skiing on New Year's Day, make a snowman family on the day of the first snowfall, and so on.
			*	Create a memory box for your child. It could include a copy of the newspaper for the day he or she was born; coins from the year he or she was born; calendars for the first few years, with notes on special events marked on the calendar (first steps, first smile, and so on); a special photo album with duplicates of special pictures; and so on.
*		*	*	Create a family photo album. After creating family and individual child albums, leave them in a prominent place where they can be easily viewed.
*		*	*	Gather and organize your photos as a family. Create one family scrapbook or provide an album for each of the children and divide the pictures up among the children to put in their album. Tell stories of your memories and experiences as you put the scrapbooks together.
			*	Pull out the family photo albums and ask each member of the family to find one memory that he or she wants to share with the family. Take turns talking about the memory, using the photos as your "show and tell."
*			*	Create a family tradition of making and viewing home movies. Show the family videos on a special night. "Sell" tickets to the production, and include popcorn and treats. Show videos of when the children were younger and the husband and wife were younger-looking.

Sense of Purpose (*continued*)

Best Practice	High Travel Solution	Spouse Focused	Children Focused	Action Item
			*	Use video in creative ways to capture family memories. For example, tape your children as they read stories to their grandparents or younger siblings, interview family members, recite poems, or act in home dramas.
				Videotape grandparents as the entire family watches a slide show or videotape of family memories. Capture their comments and memories of the events on the videotape.
				Write questions and place them in a hat for the grandparents to answer: favorite memory, favorite food, funniest experience, separate versions of their first meeting and first date, life when they were first married, first job, and so on.
				Ask grandparents to make audio- or videotapes on which they tell stories, recite poems, sing songs, and so on. Play the tapes for the children on a regular basis.
			*	Take a tradition inventory. Have someone act as scribe. As a family, list as many of your traditions as you can recall. Review your list and discuss how much you enjoy these traditions. As a family, decide if there are any traditions that need to be changed or eliminated. Put a star next to any you'd like to do more often. List any new traditions you'd like to add as a family.
		*	*	Make a "special person" meal. During dinner together as a family, select one of the family members to be singled out for special recognition. The event being recognized may be doing well on a test, accomplishing a personal goal, playing in a sports event, or anything involving extra effort. It may also be to simply recognize someone for being a special part of the family. Make a special meal, perhaps a favorite of the person who is being honored. Tie balloons to the back of the person's chair or place an unusual hat on his or her head. Express appreciation for the person and specifically acknowledge why he or she is being recognized.

Sense of Purpose (*continued*)

Best Practice	High Travel Solution	Spouse Focused	Children Focused	**Action Item**
		*	*	Make breakfast in bed for your spouse and/or children on special occasions. On a family member's birthday, serve him or her breakfast in bed. Make breakfast in bed for no particular reason.
			*	Volunteer at school. Take a break during lunch and spend some time with your child in the classroom or on the playground. Volunteer to be a room assistant or to teach the class about your profession or occupation during part of the class time. Ask the teacher if there are things that you could do at home to help the class. Let your child see you performing the work you're doing for the class.
			*	Involve children in the care of grandparents or disabled siblings.
			*	Give treats to someone. Make cookies or other treats and visit neighbors or friends of your children.
			*	Play "cookie phantom." Make cookies together as a family, put the cookies on plates, place a plate of cookies with a nice note on the doorstep of a friend, then ring the doorbell and hide.
				Have a "Make Your Day Brighter Night." As a family, make a list of friends or relatives. From the list, select one person who might benefit from an expression of love or appreciation. Have each family member write a letter expressing a positive experience that he or she recalls having had with the person. Identify specific characteristics of the person that are appreciated. Mention experiences that were humorous or enjoyable. Package all of the letters together in a special envelope or with a plate of cookies and deliver the package.
			*	On special occasions (e.g., a child going away to college, a sixteenth birthday, or a pre-wedding celebration), present a "This Is Your Life" program. Review videos and or photos ahead .

Sense of Purpose (*continued*)

Best Practice	High Travel Solution	Spouse Focused	Children Focused	Action Item
				of time and present them to the family as you describe the person's life. If this is done prior to a wedding, invite the fiancée and new in-laws to participate.
				Hold a family council and discuss the feelings each member of the family would express if it were the last time they would see each other. Ask individual members to write their thoughts on note cards prior to the discussion.
		*	*	Share your life goals and values with your family. Discuss what is most important to you and your family. Talk about your personal goals for self-improvement and character development.
		*	*	Talk about why and how your values and goals have been shaped through your experiences in life. Share experiences that have taught you valuable lessons.
				Memorize and discuss famous quotations and sayings that teach values. For example, identify and memorize as a family such quotations as "Correction does much, but encouragement does more" (Johann Wolfgang von Goethe), or "Without courage there cannot be truth, and without truth there can be no other virtue" (Sir Walter Scott), or "Anger is the wind that blows out the lamp of the mind" (Robert G. Ingersoll).
				Go to the library as a family and check out a book of quotations for each member of the family. Have family members find sayings that hold particular meaning for them personally. Post the quotations on the wall and quiz each family member on how well she or he has memorized them.
		*		Set aside time each week for you and your spouse to pursue a hobby or a personal interest.
			*	During Christmas or Hanukkah, have each member of the family take one of the gifts that she or he received and give it to a person or child who is less fortunate.

Sense of Purpose (*continued*)

Best Practice	High Travel Solution	Spouse Focused	Children Focused	Action Item
			*	Schedule vacation time to baby-sit your grand-children. Talk with their parents (your children) about what values and perspectives they want you to help them teach their children.
			*	Play "Remember When?" Give each member of the family a 3" x 5" card and ask her or him to write for 5 minutes on one or more funny and memorable events in the family. Have family members describe their "Remember When?" events one at a time in a round-robin style until all the events on the cards have been shared with the family.
			*	Offer to arrange a service project for your child's class at school.
			*	Create a special family project that everyone will enjoy. Projects could include creating a play area at home, building a swing set, building a tree house, creating a garden, and so on.
			*	Encourage work and contribution by linking a fun family activity with the accomplishment of a special work project. For example, go to an amusement park if the family will clean up the garage together.
		*	*	Celebrate Valentine's Day as a family with a candlelight dinner, followed by distributing flowers to the occupants of a nursing home. Or celebrate Mother's Day as a family, followed by visiting a nursing home and talking to the elderly women in the center.
				Celebrate the Fourth of July or Memorial Day by watching a patriotic video from the video store. For example, ask for videos made by PBS on patriotic topics.
			*	Play the "Ungame" (by Talicor, Inc.) with your family. The Ungame is a noncompetitive card game with a question on each card that requires the family member to respond to some unusual and interesting questions.

Sense of Purpose (*continued*)

Best Practice	High Travel Solution	Spouse Focused	Children Focused	Action Item
			*	Create a tradition of occasionally being a "secret pal," such as around Valentine's Day. Place the names of the family members in a hat, have them take turns drawing a name, and give them 1 week to do as many special, anonymous acts of kindness and service as possible to the person they chose. The purpose is to keep the secret pal a secret until the following week, when everyone gets to guess who her or his secret pal was.

Compliments, Builds, Encourages

Best Practice	High Travel Solution	Spouse Focused	Children Focused	Action Item
*			*	Encourage the development of good friendships by inviting your children's friends to participate in family activities and vacations.
*		*		Plan for your spouse's personal development. Allow time for him or her to pursue individual interests and personal rejuvenation.
	*		*	Recognize accomplishments every day. Ask your children questions about their activities until you can find an accomplishment to reinforce. Recognize large and small accomplishments. This activity can take place over the phone when you are traveling.
			*	Implement the Marble Jar. Find a jar that holds about 40 or 50 marbles. Place a marble in the jar each time someone in the family does something that deserves recognition or a compliment (e.g., giving service to someone else, resolving a problem without getting angry, or helping without being asked). Make sure that everyone in the family knows why the marble is being placed in the jar. This approach is particularly helpful in "reprogramming" parents to look for and recognize good behavior in their children. In addition, if children are allowed to place marbles

Complements, Builds, Encourages (*continued*)

Best Practice	High Travel Solution	Spouse Focused	Children Focused	Action Item
				in the jar for their siblings, they can be taught to recognize and compliment good behavior. When the jar is full, take the family on a special outing in recognition of its efforts.
			*	Encourage the members of your family to participate in new or varied activities. Recognize when they participate in something outside their normal set of activities.
			*	Create "stretching" family activities. Select or create activities that stretch each family member's abilities or experiences, such as learning to scuba dive, rock climb, or rappel together.
			*	Create a speech contest at home and give family members 5 minutes to develop a speech on a selected topic.
			*	Tell an impromptu, made-up story by identifying the characters in the story and having each family member in turn, in a round-robin circle, add two sentences to build on the story developed by the previous people in the circle.
*		*	*	Have a compliment party. With the family all together, give each person a turn at complimenting and building up the others by sharing the positive traits that make each family member special. Write the traits mentioned by each family member on 3" x 5" cards and give a card with the collected set of compliments to each person.
*		*	*	Take an inventory of family members' strengths and talents. During a family council, have family members write down a list of their own strengths, talents, and things that they do well. They should be encouraged to list skills such as listening or being compassionate. Family members should then share their lists with the other family members. Family members can add to others' lists by pointing out other talents and abilities that they have.

Complements, Builds, Encourages (*continued*)

Best Practice	High Travel Solution	Spouse Focused	Children Focused	**Action Item**
*		*	*	Hold a family talent night. Allow and encourage each member to share a talent with the other family members.
			*	Ask a child to use his or her drawing talent to create pictures for your place of work. Ask your child to draw on themes such as "working hard," "being honest," or "helping others," or to draw pictures that are directly related to what you do at work. Hang the pictures up on the walls at work.
*		*	*	Help each member of the family (including parents) develop personal goals. Meet with each family member to discuss her or his personal goals and dreams. Write down the specific goals and objectives. Look for opportunities to support and encourage family members' reaching for their goals by offering your strengths and abilities to complement their efforts.
*		*	*	Create a family hobby that builds on talents in the family. For example, create a family singing or musical group; perform a play together; create specialty crafts; or do creative, specialty, or ethnic cooking as a family.
			*	Recognize family members for talents that they may not realize they have, such as "being a peacemaker," "smiling," "genuinely caring for others," or "taking the initiative to do chores without being reminded."
			*	Institute a "new experience challenge." Challenge family members to do something that they haven't done before. The challenge could be to learn to water ski, interview a neighbor next door and write a report about it, run a mile, do a difficult chore, eat a little of every food on their plate for 1 week, and so on. These are things that family members are capable of doing but don't feel comfortable doing. Provide a monetary incentive.

Complements, Builds, Encourages (*continued*)

Best Practice	High Travel Solution	Spouse Focused	Children Focused	Action Item
*			*	Teach your children how to study to get good grades. Spend time discussing your formula for studying. For example, if they read and then outline the key points for each chapter they read, the outline becomes the study guide just prior to tests. Or, they can write out the questions that they anticipate will be on the test, then write out the answers to those questions ahead of time.
*			*	Attend special plays and performances that teach values and discuss those values with the family. For example, attend *A Christmas Carol* and talk about the messages "mankind being our business," "not focusing on material things," and so on.

Creation of an Action Plan

After you have identified the top five behaviors that you do well, use the family council to identify one or two actions that you can take to leverage your strengths and apply them in different ways. For example, if one of your behavioral strengths is "talking with children about important activities and events," you can make sure that you do the same with your spouse. In addition, identify the five behaviors that need the most attention. Use the family council to identify one or two actions that will help you improve in the areas that need attention. For example, if you have difficulty "teaching family members to serve each other," you may want to plan a service project that allows them to feel the joy of serving others first.

Write each action in the action plan form given here, including details of when you will begin the action and how you will know whether the action is helping you develop the behavior you want. You may want to schedule another family council to discuss your progress with the family and whether the action was helpful.

Action Plan: What I Will Do	When/How Often I Will Implement the Action	How I Will Know the Action Is Effective
1.		
2.		
3.		

CHAPTER 11

Creating the Future

"God gave us memory so that we might have roses in December."
—James Mathew Barrie

LET'S FACE IT—we all want a bright, happy future with no regrets. We want to look back on a life of accomplishment in our careers and personal relationships. In the December of our lives, we want to be loved and to have loved others. Creating a happy future with no regrets takes effort. We can shape the future by healing the past and anticipating and preventing regrets in the future through the Family 360 process.

Healing the Past

Some of the most meaningful uses of Family 360 often involve healing and rebuilding relationships with members of your family—spouse and children—but also including your extended family—brothers, sisters, parents, in-laws, and so on. Often there are old wounds that have been festering for years. Perhaps the hurt came from something your husband said or did to you. Perhaps your parents did not accept your choice of lifestyle or your spouse. You may have lingering feelings of pain and hurt from something your siblings did to offend you. Perhaps you have been mistreated or taken advantage of by someone who should have loved you. Whatever the reason, Family 360 can be a useful tool for starting to rebuild some of the relationships you have with your family.

All of the questions in the Family 360 process can be completed by extended family members—mother, father, brothers, sisters, in-laws, and other close relatives. In addition, there are three questions that are specific to extended family members in the complete survey, located in Appendix A.

The whole intent of the Family 360 experience is to bring families back together, to strengthen, to unify, and to build personal and family relationships. There are many we have worked with over the years who have expressed their value in the family unit but who have let their relationships drift into a state of unhappiness. This state of discontent can happen with the core family unit, and it can happen with members of the extended family. Many want to improve conditions, but they let pride stop them from healing the wounds that have been created over the years.

The first step in the healing process is to start with yourself—to get clear about what you really want and cherish about the family. Take time to gather data, either from a survey process like the Family 360 or from other means, to get others' perceptions about how well things are going, to identify several high-leverage actions that you can take to improve current conditions, and to go after the fix. The process is all about breaking old habits and then creating or re-creating new habits that build the relationships.

Let us give you an example of one person who went through Family 360 and decided it was time to start the healing process with his own family, including his brothers and sisters.

Bill grew up in a family of nine children—six brothers and three sisters. Over the years, they experienced many challenges—death, divorce, unemployment, and struggles with children, as well as strained relationships among themselves. At times, these challenges and trials brought some of the members of the family together; at other times the trials separated them. Family members were offended and relationships strained, sometimes for years. As a result, the family that had been close while younger had drifted apart. Bill wanted something better.

> I felt that something had to be done in order to protect our family relationships, which was more important than careers, possessions, or public praise. I decided to start the process of healing with myself. Even

though I felt like I had been taken advantage of and hurt by some of the members of the family, I realized that I had done my part to hurt others and cause the family to divide. I realized that if we were to pull together again as a family I needed to start with listening and truly trying to understand other family members. It would also require me to say the tough words "I'm sorry" and ask for forgiveness for the wrongs that I had done to them over the years.

It was hard—very hard. I had some difficult conversations with my brothers and sisters. The conversations softened my heart. I felt compassion for each of them that I had not experienced for many years. The blinders on my eyes seemed to fall as I saw my family members as real people who also want to be loved, who want to be respected, and who want to be part of a family that cares and looks out for each other.

In many ways I was ashamed of my behavior over the years. I knew that I couldn't replay the past, but I could do things differently in the future that let them know that I am there for them during their trials and challenges.

The family organized a family reunion in the town where they grew up. Bill organized an early morning breakfast with his brothers in a restaurant near their old neighborhood. After breakfast the six brothers took a walk through the old neighborhood to talk about the good times they had in their youth. Bill recounted:

My oldest brother was on crutches at the time, so we decided to surprise him by getting a wheelchair so that he could go with us on the walk through "memory lane." I had no idea how much that meant to him, nor how touched he would be to have me push him all around the neighborhood. I felt good inside. We told lots of stories about our growing years, and we laughed and hugged.

I'm sure some of the residents wondered what was happening to the neighborhood when six older men, all in their 40s and 50s, walked down the middle of the street at 7 A.M., laughing and having a good time. We finally arrived at the house that we grew up in. The memories started to flood out of our mouths as we told stories of growing up in the neighborhood. We decided to knock on the door and were even so bold as to ask the occupants if we could walk through their (our) house to reminisce.

The first thing we felt upon entering the house was how small it seemed now—how did we fit nine active kids within the walls of the tiny home. We saw some of the things that we had done to the home some 30 years ago. I even noticed the hole, in the shape of my foot, in the bathroom door, which I had made because my brother had tried to push my head in the toilet. Someone had covered it over, but the memories were still very vivid. We saw the basketball backboard and hoop that our father had made for us boys to play ball together. We went out into the backyard and saw where we had played ball, army, and fort. We talked about the memories for several hours.

By the end of the experience something had happened to us. We realized how much we loved each other, how we were family, and how important it was to forgive and mend past offenses.

My brothers and I grew up that day. We realized that pride had crept into our relationships and had robbed us of what was really important in life. We realized that it is never too late to strengthen and rebuild our relationships.

Preventing Regrets

Roger is a 39-year-old executive with seven children. He has risen to the top of his corporation in a series of rapid promotions. Roger is in a unique position because he still has "runway left"; there is time for him to rise even farther. His capabilities have not been used to his full capacity yet. Interestingly, Roger has been able to enjoy his success while raising seven children.

He puts in a significant amount of time at work and a significant amount of time with his children. He leaves early in the morning to arrive at work around 6:30 A.M. and usually returns 12 hours later. Weekends involve working with the children, helping with homework, and helping with chores around the house. He has an amazingly close relationship with his wife and children. The children feel his love and quickly say that he is "respectful of Mom all the time and shows his love to her all the time." Roger and his wife have regular "dates," and they also take the time to do things with the children as a family.

But a dangerous intersection is coming; a potential collision course is nearing. The Family 360 process raised the topic of conversation as a couple— "how much is enough?" "At what point will work really start to deteriorate the relationship at home?" At the same time, the children are getting older, and teenage independence has created a bit of an edge at home. At what point does success in one area start to diminish success in the other? That is the question Roger and his wife are wrestling with.

Creating the future will not be easy. Roger needs to spend more one-on-one time with his children and have some of the same personal conversations he had in the past—at the same time that he is experiencing growing demands on his time at work.

But Roger and his wife are talking. They are having the conversation now. They are involving the children in their discussions of how much is enough. Roger is making good use of a powerful resource in the family—the ideas and love generated from an already close family. They will get the answers they are looking for because they are talking about the dilemma and the solution— now, when it is not of crisis proportions.

In addition, they are searching for ideas with greater leverage, including how to best use the sliver of time they currently have together. Roger is committed to more one-on-one time with his children, especially during the next few years. "I realize that I only have 3 years until one daughter leaves our home. Another has 4 years, and the rest are right behind them. That is not much more time to try and make a difference." Finally, he and his wife realize that at some point they may have to make a difficult choice, one that places the family on a higher level. This will not be an either/or choice that eliminates work altogether or sends them packing to live on a farm, but a decision to not take on a new assignment or a new location. They realize it's a decision that will send a message through more than one generation—that family really is important.

Creating the future as Bill and Roger are doing, by mending the past or preventing regrets, are all possible if we understand a few principles about going through the personal change process of Family 360:

1. ***The change processes can be long and difficult.*** The journey of building stronger relationships is not easy, but it is rewarding. It is very much about taking two steps forward and one step back. *Direction and progress are more important than velocity.*

2. ***The first step may require humility.*** You may have to swallow your pride, say you're sorry, even if you were not wrong in the first place. Bill realized he was the source of some of the problem and had to humbly initiate the discussion with, and apologize to, family members. Roger needs to recognize the challenge ahead, which has been slowly, quietly building, and continue to find the right answers.

3. ***The process of creating the future requires a focus on doing a few things better.*** We have observed many people who are very interested in improving their personal and family relationships. All those who have participated in the Family 360 process have identified numerous things they can do differently to be better spouses, partners, parents, sons and daughters, and brothers and sisters. We are energized that there are so many people who want to strengthen their relationship with those whom they love. However, many will try to take on too many things at once. An individual can only work on only a few actions at a time, especially if these actions require some emotional investment. Those who try to do too much end up making very little progress. It is difficult to break away from old practices and create new habits. We can't just pick a solution from the book and fix the relationship overnight. We need to work on just a few behaviors at a time and master them to the point at which we see real progress in closing the gap between our current behavior and the legacy that we want to leave with our family.

4. ***Prepare to see some resistance.*** Change causes tension within us because we are breaking from old practices and forming new habits. This tension almost always brings with it resistance. Be prepared to see some form of resistance—from you or from others—poke its ugly head out and try to discourage you from making the transition.

5. *Involve others in the transition process.* The power of family members is enormous. They can be your strongest advocates and coaches for change throughout the personal change process, until eventually you see little of the old, and the new is fully ushered in as a permanent habit. We feel strongly that holding a "family council," even if it is with only one other person, is vitally important to your improvement efforts. As Roger is doing, let your family know what you are going to work on, allow them to understand the old behavior that you are trying to change, explain in very specific terms the new way you desire to behave, and tell them of your need for their loving and reinforcing feedback along the way. Let them know that you will not automatically change overnight, like turning off a valve. You will make mistakes. In fact, you may actually demonstrate the new behavior, and no one may notice your efforts. They may even react in a way as if you had just demonstrated the old behavior. You will be standing there with amazement saying, "Hey, I just did it the new way, and you didn't even notice." That's okay, and it should be expected. Remember, they have been programmed to react to an old behavior that they have seen for years. They will have to change how they react to your new behavior too, which is another reason why it is important to let others that you love know what you are trying to change so that you can work together.

In summary, we are talking about personal change, not changing your family, your spouse, or your children, but changing your own heart and mind and behavior. It includes 1) identifying current state and future state (family legacy), 2) determining how to close the gap, and 3) taking meaningful action to build and maintain great personal and family relationships. Taking these steps will result in getting your family to talk, solve problems, and improve relationships.

> *"To put the world right in order, we must first put the nation in order; to put the nation in order, we must first put the family in order; to put the family in order, we must first cultivate our personal life; we must first set our hearts right."*
>
> —Confucius

As we have communicated to others in the past, "It is never too late." Good luck!

Tell Us about the Activities
That Help You Strengthen
Your Personal and Family Relationships

We are interested in hearing from you about what works well in your family. We would like to add to our list of best practices.

1. What activities do you consider to be your own best practices?

  - What activities have helped you communicate more effectively as a family?
  - What activities have helped your family members grow in their relationships with one another?
  - What activities have become meaningful family traditions?
  - What activities have helped members of your family to serve others?

2. What activities have helped you stay close to your family, despite your heavy travel schedule?

3. What activities have helped you and your spouse or partner grow closer as a couple?

4. What activities have helped you grow closer to your children?

  - What activities have helped your family stay together even after the children have left the home?

We appreciate your sharing your best practices with us—to provide more ideas for coaching other busy people. Send your ideas and experiences to Leader-Works at the following locations.

Email: ben@leaderworks.net

Address:

LeaderWorks
17185 Colonial Park Drive
Monument, CO 80132

Family 360 Survey

Communication and Listening

	Needs Significant Attention	Needs Some Attention	Almost Acceptable	Acceptable	More than Acceptable	Strength	Significant Strength
1. Is patient with family members	O	O	O	O	O	O	O
2. Openly talks about important things	O	O	O	O	O	O	O
3. Takes time to have personal conversations	O	O	O	O	O	O	O
4 Listens to what others have to say	O	O	O	O	O	O	O
5. Pays attention to personal feelings when communicating	O	O	O	O	O	O	O
6. Openly talks about what he or she has learned from his or her mistakes	O	O	O	O	O	O	O

Communication and Listening (*continued*)

	Needs Significant Attention	Needs Some Attention	Almost Acceptable	Acceptable	More than Acceptable	Strength	Significant Strength
7. Is fair and consistent with family members	O	O	O	O	O	O	O
Problem Solving							
8. Seeks fair solutions to problems	O	O	O	O	O	O	O
9. Helps resolve disagreements to everyone's satisfaction	O	O	O	O	O	O	O
10. Solves problems without getting angry or keeping silent	O	O	O	O	O	O	O
Support							
11. Works hard to provide food and a home for the family	O	O	O	O	O	O	O
12. Makes sure that all family members' needs are met	O	O	O	O	O	O	O
13. Helps family members feel safe and secure at home	O	O	O	O	O	O	O

Equal Partnership and Respect

	Needs Significant Attention	Needs Some Attention	Almost Acceptable	Acceptable	More than Acceptable	Strength	Significant Strength
14. Recognizes and respects spouse's role in the home	O	O	O	O	O	O	O
15. Recognizes and respects spouse's job role	O	O	O	O	O	O	O
16. Shares fairly in rearing children	O	O	O	O	O	O	O
17. Shares home chores fairly	O	O	O	O	O	O	O

Demonstrating Love

	Needs Significant Attention	Needs Some Attention	Almost Acceptable	Acceptable	More than Acceptable	Strength	Significant Strength
18. Says "I love you" often enough	O	O	O	O	O	O	O
19. Shows love by the things he or she does	O	O	O	O	O	O	O
20. Creates an environment of love when together	O	O	O	O	O	O	O
21. Uses a kind voice when speaking	O	O	O	O	O	O	O
22. Makes others feel important	O	O	O	O	O	O	O

Family 360

Demonstrating Love (*continued*)

	Needs Significant Attention	Needs Some Attention	Almost Acceptable	Acceptable	More than Acceptable	Strength	Significant Strength
23. Is a true friend	O	O	O	O	O	O	O
24. Kindly respects differences of opinion	O	O	O	O	O	O	O
25. Talks with children about their important events and activities (i.e., school work, etc.)	O	O	O	O	O	O	O

Integrity

26. Keeps promises	O	O	O	O	O	O	O
27. Apologizes when he or she has done something wrong or has hurt others' feelings	O	O	O	O	O	O	O
28. Encourages everyone to participate in making family decisions	O	O	O	O	O	O	O
29. Keeps a secret when asked	O	O	O	O	O	O	O

Dedication of Time

	Needs Significant Attention	Needs Some Attention	Almost Acceptable	Acceptable	More than Acceptable	Strength	Significant Strength
30. Spends unhurried time with family members	O	O	O	O	O	O	O
31. Does fun things with family members	O	O	O	O	O	O	O
32. Spends regular one-on-one time with family members (e.g., dates, heart-to-heart talks, etc.)	O	O	O	O	O	O	O
33. Is flexible in his or her schedule to spend time with family members	O	O	O	O	O	O	O
34. Spends time with the children doing things they enjoy	O	O	O	O	O	O	O
35. Spends time with the children when they need help	O	O	O	O	O	O	O

Family 360

Dedication of Time (*continued*)

	Needs Significant Attention	Needs Some Attention	Almost Acceptable	Acceptable	More than Acceptable	Strength	Significant Strength
36. Participates in the children's important events and activities	O	O	O	O	O	O	O
37. Encourages weekly "date night" with spouse	O	O	O	O	O	O	O

Fun and Humor

38. Has a way of making things more fun and enjoyable	O	O	O	O	O	O	O
39. Initiates fun recreational activities	O	O	O	O	O	O	O
40. Has a sense of humor that is appreciated	O	O	O	O	O	O	O

Sense of Purpose

41. Helps the family to be united	O	O	O	O	O	O	O
42. Shows by his or her actions that the family is more important than other aspects of life (e.g., work, hobbies, civic responsibilities)	O	O	O	O	O	O	O

Appendix A

Sense of Purpose (*continued*)

	Needs Significant Attention	Needs Some Attention	Almost Acceptable	Acceptable	More than Acceptable	Strength	Significant Strength
43. Encourages family members to help and serve others	O	O	O	O	O	O	O
44. Encourages family members to work together	O	O	O	O	O	O	O
45. Helps create enjoyable family traditions (birthdays, holidays, etc.)	O	O	O	O	O	O	O
46. Teaches the children moral values	O	O	O	O	O	O	O
47. Teaches the children responsibility and accountability	O	O	O	O	O	O	O
48. Encourages children to obey the law	O	O	O	O	O	O	O
49. Encourages children to work	O	O	O	O	O	O	O

Compliments, Builds, Encourages

	Needs Significant Attention	Needs Some Attention	Almost Acceptable	Acceptable	More than Acceptable	Strength	Significant Strength
50. Shows confidence in family member's abilities to perform well in various aspects of life (e.g., work, school, sports)	O	O	O	O	O	O	O
51. Compliments family members for their personal achievements	O	O	O	O	O	O	O
52. Gives family members credit for their personal accomplishments	O	O	O	O	O	O	O
53. Helps family members improve their talents	O	O	O	O	O	O	O
54. Encourages family members to keep trying when they are having trouble accomplishing a task	O	O	O	O	O	O	O

Compliments, Builds, Encourages (*continued*)

	Needs Significant Attention	Needs Some Attention	Almost Acceptable	Acceptable	More than Acceptable	Strength	Significant Strength
55. Is kind toward family members when they do something wrong	O	O	O	O	O	O	O
Extended Family Feedback							
56. Communicates via email or phone on a regular basis	O	O	O	O	O	O	O
57. Encourages the extended family to do things together	O	O	O	O	O	O	O
58. Forgives past mistakes of individual family members	O	O	O	O	O	O	O

Family 360 Results Calculation Form/Action Plan

Question #	Scores (Write the scores from the cards onto this form.)					Average Score (Write your average score.)	Top 5 or Bottom 5 (Select only the Top 5 or Bottom 5)	Category of Question	Best Practices (See pages in the Best Practices section)
Example: 1. Is patient with family members	5	4	4	6	3	4.4	Bottom 5	*Communication and Listening*	*Ideas for Communication and Listening are on pages of the Best Practice Guide*

Write your data in the spaces below.

Question #	Scores					Average Score	Top 5 or Bottom 5	Category of Question	Best Practices
1. Is patient with family members								Communication and Listening	Ideas are located in Chapter 8
2. Openly talks about important things								Communication and Listening	Ideas are located in Chapter 8
3. Takes time to have personal conversations								Communication and Listening	Ideas are located in Chapter 8

Family 360 Results Calculation Form (*continued*)

Question #	Scores					Average Score	Top 5 or Bottom 5	Category of Question	Best Practices
4. Listens to what others have to say								Communication and Listening	Ideas are located in Chapter 8
5. Pays attention to personal feelings when com-municating								Communication and Listening	Ideas are located in Chapter 8
6. Openly talks about what he or she has learned from his or her mistakes								Communication and Listening	Ideas are located in Chapter 8
7. Is fair and consistent with family members								Communication and Listening	Ideas are located in Chapter 8
8. Seeks fair solutions to problems								Problem Solving	Ideas are located in Chapter 8
9. Helps resolve disagree-ments to everyone's satisfaction								Problem Solving	Ideas are located in Chapter 8
10. Solves problems without getting angry or keeping silent								Problem Solving	Ideas are located in Chapter 8

Family 360 Results Calculation Form (*continued*)

Question #	Scores					Average Score	Top 5 or Bottom 5	Category of Question	Best Practices
11. Works hard to provide food and a home for the family								Support	Ideas are located in Chapter 8
12. Makes sure that all family members' needs are met								Support	Ideas are located in Chapter 8
13. Helps family members feel safe and secure at home								Support	Ideas are located in Chapter 8
14. Recognizes and respects spouse's role in the home								Equal Partnership and Respect	Ideas are located in Chapter 8
15. Recognizes and respects spouse's job role								Equal Partnership and Respect	Ideas are located in Chapter 8
16. Shares fairly in rearing children								Equal Partnership and Respect	Ideas are located in Chapter 8
17. Shares home chores fairly								Equal Partnership and Respect	Ideas are located in Chapter 8
18. Says "I love you" often enough								Demonstrating Love	Ideas are located in Chapter 9

Family 360 Results Calculation Form (*continued*)

Question #	Scores					Average Score	Top 5 or Bottom 5	Category of Question	Best Practices
19. Shows love by the things he or she does								Demonstrating Love	Ideas are located in Chapter 9
20. Creates an environment of love when together								Demonstrating Love	Ideas are located in Chapter 9
21. Uses a kind voice when speaking								Demonstrating Love	Ideas are located in Chapter 9
22. Makes others feel important								Demonstrating Love	Ideas are located in Chapter 9
23. Is a true friend								Demonstrating Love	Ideas are located in Chapter 9
24. Kindly respects differences of opinion								Demonstrating Love	Ideas are located in Chapter 9
25. Talks with children about their important events and activities (i.e., schoolwork, etc.)								Demonstrating Love	Ideas are located in Chapter 9
26. Keeps promises								Integrity	Ideas are located in Chapter 9
27. Apologizes when he or she has done something wrong or has hurt others' feelings								Integrity	Ideas are located in Chapter 9

Family 360 Results Calculation Form (*continued*)

Question #	Scores					Average Score	Top 5 or Bottom 5	Category of Question	Best Practices
28. Encourages everyone to participate in making family decisions								Integrity	Ideas are located in Chapter 9
29. Keeps a secret when asked								Integrity	Ideas are located in Chapter 9
30. Spends unhurried time with family members								Demonstrating Love	Ideas are located in Chapter 9
31. Does fun things with family members								Demonstrating Love	Ideas are located in Chapter 9
32. Spends regular one-on-one time with family members (e.g., dates, heart-to-heart talks, etc.)								Demonstrating Love	Ideas are located in Chapter 9
33. Is flexible in his or her schedule to spend time with family members								Demonstrating Love	Ideas are located in Chapter 9
34. Spends time with the children doing things they enjoy								Demonstrating Love	Ideas are located in Chapter 9

Family 360 Results Calculation Form (*continued*)

Question #	Scores						Average Score	Top 5 or Bottom 5	Category of Question	Best Practices
35. Spends time with the children when they need help									Demonstrating Love	Ideas are located in Chapter 9
36. Participates in the children's important events and activities									Demonstrating Love	Ideas are located in Chapter 9
37. Encourages weekly "date night" with spouse									Demonstrating Love	Ideas are located in Chapter 9
38. Has a way of making things more fun and enjoyable									Fun and Humor	Ideas are located in Chapter 9
39. Initiates fun recreational activities									Fun and Humor	Ideas are located in Chapter 9
40. Has a sense of humor that is appreciated									Fun and Humor	Ideas are located in Chapter 9
41. Helps the family to be united									Sense of Purpose	Ideas are located in Chapter 10

Family 360 Results Calculation Form (*continued*)

Question #	Scores					Average Score	Top 5 or Bottom 5	Category of Question	Best Practices
42. Shows by his or her actions that the family is more important than other aspects of life (e.g., work, hobbies, civic responsibilities)								Sense of Purpose	Ideas are located in Chapter 10
43. Encourages family members to help and serve others								Sense of Purpose	Ideas are located in Chapter 10
44. Encourages family members to work together								Sense of Purpose	Ideas are located in Chapter 10
45. Helps create enjoyable family traditions (birthdays, holidays, etc.)								Sense of Purpose	Ideas are located in Chapter 10
46. Teaches the children moral values								Sense of Purpose	Ideas are located in Chapter 10
47. Teaches the children responsibility and accountability								Sense of Purpose	Ideas are located in Chapter 10

Family 360 Results Calculation Form (*continued*)

Question #	Scores					Average Score	Top 5 or Bottom 5	Category of Question	Best Practices
48 Encourages children to obey the law								Sense of Purpose	Ideas are located in Chapter 10
49. Encourages children to work								Sense of Purpose	Ideas are located in Chapter 10
50. Shows confidence in family member's abilities to perform well in various aspects of life (e.g., work, school, or sports)								Compliments, Builds and Encourages	Ideas are located in Chapter 10
51 Compliments family members for their personal achievements								Compliments, Builds and Encourages	Ideas are located in Chapter 10
52. Gives family members credit for their personal accomplishments								Compliments, Builds and Encourages	Ideas are located in Chapter 10
53. Helps family members improve their talents								Compliments, Builds and Encourages	Ideas are located in Chapter 10

Family 360 Results Calculation Form (*continued*)

Question #	Scores					Average Score	Top 5 or Bottom 5	Category of Question	Best Practices
54. Encourages family members to keep trying when they are having trouble accomplishing a task								Compliments, Builds and Encourages	Ideas are located in Chapter 10
55. Is kind toward family members when they do something wrong								Compliments, Builds and Encourages	Ideas are located in Chapter 10
Extended Family Questions									
56. Communicates via email or phone on a regular basis								Extended Family	
57. Encourages the extended family to do things together								Extended Family	
58. Forgives past mistakes of individual family members								Extended Family	

Action Plan: What I Will Do	When/How Often I Will Implement the Action	How I Will Know the Action Is Effective
1.		
2.		
3.		

Index

About the Authors

PERRY M. CHRISTENSEN has 23 years of senior human resource experience, holding executive-level human resource positions at Merck, WFD Consulting, and Celanese. He has consulted and coached many *Fortune* 100 company executives from around the world—Japan, Singapore, Australia, South Africa, and most countries in Europe—on work/life practices and company policies. Perry has conducted research in collaboration with the Wharton Business School on leadership competencies and work/life integration strategies. His work on balancing work and life has resulted in two articles in the *Harvard Business Review*, a book published by Jossey-Bass entitled *Integrating Work and Life: The Wharton Resource Guide*, and several other articles and book chapters.

BENSON L. PORTER has 22 years of "real world" executive coaching and development experience and has held executive-level positions at Lockheed, Amoco, PepsiCo, and AlliedSignal, where he was vice president of organization and leadership development and the company's chief learning officer. He is currently founder and president of LeaderWorks, an executive coaching and development firm based in Colorado, which is focused on helping organizations to build executive capability. Ben has coached thousands of executives from all over the world, and he has designed and runs the executive development programs for companies such as General Motors, Honeywell, and Eaton.